SIKHS

SIKHS

Captain A. H. Bingley

KALPAZ

ISBN: 978-93-5128-587-8

First Published in 1899
Indian Reprint in 2017

Published by

Kalpaz Publications
C-30, Satyawati Nagar,
Delhi – 110052
E-mail: kalpaz@hotmail.com
Website: kalpazpublications.com
Ph.: +91-9212142040

Cataloging in Publication Data--DK
Courtesy: D.K. Agencies (P) Ltd. <docinfo@dkagencies.com>

Cataloging in Publication Data--DK
Courtesy: D.K. Agencies (P) Ltd. <docinfo@dkagencies.com>

Bingley, A. H., 1865-1944, author.
Sikhs / Captain A.H. Bingley.
pages cm
"First published in 1899"--Title page verso.
ISBN 9789351285878 (HB)

1. Sikhs. I. Title.

DS432.S5B55 2017 DDC 306.0882946 23

INDEX TO HAND BOOK ON SIKHS.

CONTENTS.

PAGES

CHAPTER I.—History and origin ... ... 1—28

A

Abchalnagar 19
Adam Háfiz 15
Afgháns, conflicts of—with Jats 10
Afghánistán, Aryan occupation of— 2
Agnicular Rájpúts, origin of— 8
Agricultural classes, origin of— 3, 4
Ahmad Shah, invasions of— 20
Ajudhya 7
Akális 23
Ala Singh, of Patiála 21
Aliwál, battle of— 26
Amr Dás, 3rd Gúrú 12, 14
Amritsar, sanctity of— 14
Anandpur 16
Arjún, 5th Gúrú 12, 14
Army, formation of—by Ranjit Singh 24
——, reorganization of—after Mutiny 28
Aryans, early history of the— 2, 3, 4
——, original home of the— 2
——, conditions of life among the— 2
——, organization of the—into four classes 3
Aurangzéb 10
Avatars 7
Awáns 10

B

Bábar 10
Bactrians, invasions of— 7
Bairagi, definition of— 19
Balúchis 11
Banda, Govind Singh's successor 19
Bhattinda 18
Bhúmia 9

PAGES

CHAPTER I—*contd.*

Bódi, or scalp lock 13
Bráhma 5
Brahmas 3
Bráhmans, origin of— 2, 3
Bráhmanism, revival of— 5, 6
————, assimilative character of— 7
Buddhism 5
————, influence of—on Sikhism 12
————, spread of—throughout Asia 6
————, absorption of—by Bráhmanism 7

C

Caste, definition of— 3
————, origin of— 3, 4, 5
————, rejection of—by Buddhism 5
————, restrictions of—imposed by Dharma Shástras ... 6
————, rules, absence of—in Sikhism 13
Chhatri, Chhatriya, Kshatriya, Rájpút, or Thákúr ... 3, 4
Chillianwala, battle of— 26
Chóti, or scalp lock 13

D

Dalip Singh, Máharája 25
Dal Khalsa, or Sikh army 23
Dam Damma, or Gúrú's breathing place 18
Dekhan, Sikh colonies of the— 19
Dérajat 26
Dévi or Débi 16
Dharma-Shástras 6
Discus, or quoit, use of the—by Jats 9

E

Edwardes, Herbert 27

F

Ferozepore, the Sikh regiment of— 27, 28
Firozshahr, battle of— 26
Foreign Officers, employment of—by Ranjit Singh ... 24

G

Gakkars 10
Getæ or Goths 1
Ghazni, connection of Jats, with— 8, 9
Govind Singh, 10th Gúrú 12
————————, death of— 19
————————, employment of — by Mughals ... 18

PAGES

CHAPTER I— *contd.*

Govind Singh, life and policy of— 16
————, quarrels of—with Sódhis 17
————, struggles of—with Mughals 18
————, the successor of— 19
Granth, Adi 14
————, Daswén-Badshah-ki 18
Greeks, invasions of the— 7
Guides, the Corps of—when raised 27
Gújars 8
Gújar women, concubinage of— 9
Gujrat, battle of— 26
Gúrús, list of the ten 12

H

Har Govind, 6th Gúrú 12, 14
Hari Singh 24
Har Rai, 7th Gúrú 12, 15
Har Kishn, 8th Gúrú 12, 15
Hinduism, modern, origin of— 6
Hindki 11
Hungarians 1

I

Indus 2
Invasions of Ahmad Shah 20
———— of Bactrians 7
———— of Greeks 7
———— of Nádir Shah 19, 20, 23
Islám, influence of—on Sikhism 12

J

Jádu or Yadu 1, 8, 9
Janjúas 10
Jats, attacks of—on Mahmúd of Ghazni 10
——, captivity of—in Ghazni 10
——, connection of—with Magyars and Gypsies ... 1
————, ————, with Rájpúts 1
————, ————, with Scythians 1, 7, 8, 9
————, conversion of—to Hinduism 8
————, ———— to Islám 10
——, defeat of—by Mahmúd of Ghazni 10
——, descent of— 9
——, difference between—and Rájpúts 8
——, geographical distribution of— 7
——, legends of the— 8, 9
—— of the Central Punjáb—their characteristics ... 11
—— of the Western Punjáb—their characteristics ... 10, 11
—— of Rájpútána,—their defeat by the Rájpúts ... 12
——, origin of the— 1, 7
——, rise of the—due to Musalmán persecutions ... 12
——, their republicanism 11, 12

		Pages
Chapter I—*contd.*	Jatta	9
	Jahángir	14
	Jowáhir Singh	25
	Jumna	5, 6, 7

K

Kangra 26
Kanouj 12
Karao, Karéwa, or widow-marriage 8, 9
Kartarpur 12
Kasabgótra 9
Kashmir 26
Khálsa, definition of the term— 15, 16, 20
———, democratic tendencies of the— 16, 17
———, army of the—its composition 23
———, conversion of—into regulars 24
———, conditions of service in the— 24
———, revival of—during the Mutiny 28
——— army, defeat of—by British 25, 26
—————, European officers in the— 24
—————, influence of pancháyats in— 25
—————, usurpation of power by the— ... 25
Kshatriya— 3, 4, 6
Khwas, or concubines 9
Khúsru 14
Koh-i-Núr, capture of—by Nádir Shah 23

L

Lahore, occupation of—by Sikhs and Afgháns ... 22
———, Rájpút rule of— 8
———, repulse of Akális at—by British Sepoys ... 24
Lake, victories of 23
Lawrence, his influence—in the Punjáb 27, 28
Loyalty of Punjáb in 1857 27
——— of Sikhs in Mutiny 28
Lúdhiána Sikhs 27
Lunar Race 7

M

Magyars 1
Máháréjas 2, 3, 4
Mahmúd of Ghazni 10
Mahájan, definition of— 8
Mahrattas 12, 19, 20, 21
Mansúr Ráo 8

		PAGES
CHAPTER I—*contd.*	Mánu, Institutes of—	6
	Máraj, Máharáj or—Phulkián states	11, 12
	Mathura	7
	Mazbhi Sikhs, origin of	15
	Misls, or Sikh confederacies—rise of the —	20, 21
	Mokhan Chand	24
	Mooltan	10, 26
	Mudki, battle of—	26
	Mughal Empire, decay of—	19
	Mughals, persecution of Sikhs by the—	18, 19
	Muhammad Ghori	12
	Múlraj	26
	Musalmán Jats of Western Punjab	10, 11
	————, hatred of—by Sikhs	17
	Mutiny, influence of the—on Sikhs	27, 28

N

Náderh 19

Nádir Shah, invasions of— 20, 23

Nának Bába—1st Gúrú 12

————, life and doctrines of— 12, 13

Nának-panthis 13

Nicholson 27

P

Pahúl, or Sikh oath 16

Pancháyats 25

Pánipat 20

Parméshwar... 12

Parshád, or Sikh communion 17

Patiála 18, 21

Peshávar, conquest of—by Sikhs 23

Phulkián states 12

Puránas 14

Q

Quoits, use of—by Jats 9

R

Rájpúts, Agnicular—their origin 8

————, connection of Yádu—with Jats 8

————, ——, with Jats 1

————, difference between—and Jats 8

————, intercourse of—with Jatnis and Gújarins ... 9

————, origin of—... ... ... 3, 4

————, quarrels of—with Brahmans 5

Rájkúlas, or royal tribes 9

PAGES

CHAPTER I—*contd.*

Ráma 7
Rám Dás, 4th Gúrú 12, 14
———————, his descendants 17
Ranjit Singh, Máharája—rise of— 22, 23, 24
Rattray's Sikhs 27, 28
Republicanism—of the Jats 11
Rishis 2, 3

S

Sajdháris or Nának panthis 13
Sakya Múni or Buddha, doctrines of— 5
Scythians 1, 7
———, connection of—with Jats 9
———, conversion of—to Hinduism 8
———, employment of—by Bráhmans 8
———, geographical distribution of— 7
———, invasions of— 7, 8
Serpent-worship 7
Sikh Army 23
————, conditions of service in— 24
—— baptism 17
—— communion 17
—— conquests 23
—— corps in British service 26, 27
—— insurrection—against Afgháns 20, 21
—— meaning of term 1, 13
—— wars 26
—— scriptures, compilation of— 14, 18
Sikhs, degenerate into bandits 15
—— of the Dekhan—their origin 19
—— persecutions of—by Mughals 19
—— state of society among the—in 17th century ... 22
—— services of—in Mutiny 28
Sikhism, centre of—at Amritsar 14
———, effect of—in promoting social freedom ... 17
———, military aspect of— 15
———, origin of— 12
———, outward signs of— 17
———, political aspect of— 16
———, revival of— 28
Singh 13, 17
Sirhind, capture of—by Sikhs 21
———, curse on— 21
Sirdars, causes which led to the rise of the Sikh... ... 22
———, quarrels of— 21
———, their treachery to the Khálsa 25

		PAGES
CHAPTER I—*concld.*	Siva	9
	Solar Race	6
	Sone...	2
	Sutlej, campaign of the—	26
	T	
	Trinity, the Hindu—	5
	Trading classes, origin of—	3, 4
	Totem, definition of—	7
	Tegh Bahádur, 9th Gúrú	12, 15
	Talwandi...	12, 18
	/Theocracy or Khálsa—of the Sikhs	20
	V	
	Várnas	3
	Védas	2, 4, 14
	Védism and Bráhmanism...	5
	Vaisiyas	4, 6, 17
	Vindhyas	2, 3
	Vishnu	5, 9
	Y	
	Yádu	8, 9
	Z	
	Zanánas	9
CHAPTER II.-	Classification and geographical distribution	29, 51
	A.	
	Ahlúwalia	43
	Akbar	32, 33, 36
	Aróras	40, 41
	Aulak	30, 31
	B.	
	Bains	30, 31
	Bajju or Bajwa	30, 31
	Bal	30, 31
	Bat or Bath	30, 31
	Bédhis	38, 39
	Bhular	30
	Bráhman	37
	C.	
	Chahil	30, 32
	Chaman	30, 32
	Chamár	45, 47, 48

		Pages
Chapter II—*contd.*	Chhimba	45, 46
	Chima	30, 32, 46
	Chuhra	45, 48, 49, 50
	D	
	Déo	30, 32
	Dekhani Sikhs	50
	Dháliwál, Dhániwál or Dháriwál	30, 32
	Dhillon	30, 33
	Difference between Mánjha, Málwa and Dóaba Sikhs... ...	29
	G	
	Gharéwál	30, 33
	Gil	30, 34
	Goráya	30, 34
	H	
	Her	30, 31
	Hinjra	30, 34
	Hundal	30, 34
	J	
	Jathéra	32, 33
	Jhiwar, Jhinwar, Kahár or Sakka	46
	Jógis	32
	K	
	Kahár ... ... — ...	46
	Kalál, Kalwar, or Áhlúwalia	43
	Kamboh	43
	Khaire	30, 34
	Khatri	38, 39
	Khang	30, 34
	Khosa	30, 35
	L	
	Labána	41
	M	
	Mán	30, 31
	Mahtam or Mahton	42
	N	
	Nai	45

		Pages
	P	
Chapter II—*concld.*	Pannún	30, 35
	R	
	Rájpút	37, 38
	Ramgarhia or Tarkhán	44
	Randháwa	30, 35
	Rangréta	48, 49, 50
	S	
	Sahi	30, 35
	Sahoti	30, 35
	Saini	42
	Sandhu or Sindhu	30, 36
	Sánsi	30, 35
	Sidhu	30, 36
	Sohal	30, 35
	T	
	Tarar	30, 36
	Tarkhán or Ramgarhia	44
	U	
	Uthwál or Untwál	30, 34
	V	
	Virk	30, 36
Chapter III.	Religion, Customs, Sects, Festivals, and Fairs	52—89
	A	
	Acháraj or Mahá Bráhman	78, 79
	Adi Granth	53, 54, 69
	Administering of Pahúl	71
	Age for betrothal	72
	—— for marriage	74
	Agwáni	62
	Akális	56, 59, 67
	Akál Purkh	67
	Akál Bungah	58, 79
	Amáwas	81, 88
	Amrit	78
	Anant Chaudas	82
	Ashtmi	86

		Pages
CHAPTER III—*contd.*	Asnán	88
	Ast...	79

B

Bába Farid	61
Bába Nának	52
Baisákhi	84
Baptism, ceremonies relating to—	71
Barangbári	70
Bar	61
Barát	74, 75, 80
Basanti	62
Basant Panchmi	82
Beeah	74, 76, 80
Betrothal	72
Bhairon	65
Bhaiwála or Bhaibala	82
Bharai	65
Bháts	73
Bhúmiya	60, 89
Bhúts	63, 78
Bilás	68
Bilva or Bél plant	61
Birth, ceremonies relating to—	70, 71
Birthdays of Gúrús	88, 89
Bódiwala	64
Bráhma	52, 60
Bráhmans	58, 59, 63, 69, 70, 71, 79
Breath, prohibitions regarding the—...	55
Brother's widow—marriage with a—...	77, 78

C

Canal Worship	60
Chadar dálna	77
Chandar Girhan	88
Chapátis	59
Charan gháwál	54, 71
Chédna	73
Chéla	66
Chóti or Bódi	64
Chúhara	73
Chúhra	70
Churél	63
Cow, reverence of the—	62
Customs relating to Baptism	71
——— Birth	70, 71
——— Death	78, 79, 80

		Pages
Chapter III—*contd.*	Customs relating to Marriage—	72, 73, 74, 75, 76, 77, 78

D

Darbar Sahib 54, 58, 79
Daswén Badshah ki Granth 54
Dasehra Jéth 85
Dasehra-Naoratri 87
Date of Marriages, postponement of— 75
Daughters, marriage of—... ... ... 72, 73
Decay of Sikhism 56
Deg river 60
Deváta or Nágan ka Púja... 86
Deváthri or Déoúthan 88
Dévi 62, 85
Dévi Sikhs 68
Dharmsála 59
Dharma Shástras 69, 77
Dhóti... 56
Diwáli 60, 88
Dúrga Púja 87

F

Farid, Bába 61
Five Kakkás, the— 55

G

Ganges 60, 63, 66
Gáona 76, 88
Gayáls 62
Godlings 59
Golden Temple 58
Govind Singh, doctrines and injunctions of— 54
————————, Sikhism of— 54
Granth 53
————, how kept 59
Granthis 83
Gúga Pir 61
Gulábdási 68
Gúrú, definition of— 53

I

Islám, influence of—on Nának 50
Indigo, superstitions regarding— 63

PAGES

J

CHAPTER III—*contd.*

Jandiála 65
Janéo 55
Japji 58
Jathéra 61, 89
Ját Karam 70, 80
Jats, Hinduism of — 58, 59
——, Sultáni 64
Jhand 61, 75
Jhatka 55, 56
Jógis 62
Jurah 72

K

Kabir 52
Kabir-panthis 52
Kachh 55
Kanágat 79
Karams 70, 71, 80
Karáo or Karéwa 77
Karmai 73
Khanda-dhári 55
Khande ka Pahúl 54, 56
Khéra 60
Khes 66
Khúsa 62, 79
Khwája Kizir ka Púja 60, 89
Kúkas 56, 69
Kurkhetar 79

L

Lagan 73
Lagis 73, 74, 75
Láwan 76
Leave 80

M

Mahá Bráhmans 78
Máha Mai 62
Makar Sankrant 81
Malevolent deities 62
Mangiah 73
Málwa Sikhs, Hindu tendencies of— 59
Mántras 63, 76
Mánji 59
Marriage 72, 73, 74, 75, 76, 77, 78
Masáni 62

		PAGES
CHAPTER III—*contd.*	Mauni Amáwas	81
	Mazbhis, exclusion of—from Sikh Shrines	58
	Minor injunctions—of Govind Singh	55
	Mirásis	71, 73
	Mohant	66
	Monkeys, reverence of—	62
	Moral precepts—of the Adi Granth	53
	Mourning, period of—	79
	Mughal power, hatred of—by Sikhs	56
	Mukht	53
	Mukhláwa	76
	Munna	55, 64
	Musalmán Saints, worship of—	61
	———influences,—on Sikhism	52, 63
	Mutiny, influence of—on Sikhism	56

N

Nai	73, 76
Naindhári	70
Nám Karam	71, 80
Nának, Bába—his doctrines	52
——— his views regarding transmigration ...	53
——— his birthday	88
——— his rite of baptism	54
Nának-panthi	64, 72
Naorátri	87
Nihang	67
Niranjani or Narinjani	66
Nirankari	69
Nirmalá	67
Núris	63

P

Pag	70
Pahoya	79
Pahúl......	55, 64, 65 70
Pahúlia	55
Panjgátra	84
Paróhit or Padha	71, 77
Parshád	55
Patasa	72
Patra	71
Phéra	76
Phul	79
Pinda	79, 80
Pipal	61, 80
Pirkhána or Thán	65

		Pages
Chapter III—*contd.*	Pisácha	63
	Pitrs	61
	Plague	63
	Plant worship	61
	Planet worship	61
	Postponement of marriages, effect of—	75
	Prayers, Sikh	58
	Precepts, inculcated by—the Adi Granth	53
	Préts	63
	Protestant Reformation	52
	Pun	72
	Pundit	75
	Punjáb peasants, religion of—	59
	——— saints	61

R

Rahras	58
Rájni Dévi	84
Raksha Bandhan	85
Rám Naumi	83
Rámráias	66
Reformers, Hindu	52
Rites, funeral	78, 79, 80
River worship	60, 84
Rót	65

S

Saints, Musalmán, reverence of—	61
Sainted dead, worship of—	60
Saggai	72
Sains or Gulábdásis	68
Sajdhári	64
Sakhi Sarwar	64, 84
Sánsi	71
Sects, Sikh	64—70
Sesamum, superstitions regarding—	64
Shádi or Sart	74
Shástras	67, 76
Sheorátri	82
Sherbet	72
Shraddha or Shant ceremonies	79
Sikhs, Hindu tendencies of—	59
Sikh oath, the Pahúl or—	55
—— prayers	58
—— festivals and fairs	80
Sikhism of Nának	52
———, outward signs of—	55
———, minor observances of—	55

		PAGES
CHAPTER III—*concld.*	Sikhism of Govind Singh	54
	——, decay of—	56
	——, revival of—	56
	——, present position of—	57
	——, influence of Hinduism on—	57
	Singh	55, 64
	Sitála Saptami	85
	Somwári Amáwas	88
	Sultáni	64
	Súraj Girhan	88
	T	
	Tháns	65
	Thrówa	78
	Transmigration, Nanák's doctrine regarding—	53
	Tree worship	61
	U	
	Udási	66, 67, 68
	V	
	Vallabha	52
	Vishnu	52, 59
	Village godlings	59
	W	
	Widows, marriage of—	77, 78
	Women, Sikh, inclination of—to Hinduism	57, 58
CHAPTER IV.—	Characteristics	90—105
	A	
	Abádis	103
	Ablutions among Sikhs	94
	Adoption, ceremonies and customs relating to—	104
	Africa, service of Sikhs in—	93, 95
	Agriculture in Sikh districts	105
	Akális	95
	Atris	105
	B	
	Baisákhi fair	105
	Batlóhi	[99
	Béla	99
	Bérra	97

PAGES

CHAPTER IV—*contd.*

Bhaiband or Pagband 103
Bhang, use of — by Sikhs 98
Bharóla 102
Bhistis 98
Burma, service of Sikhs in— 93, 95

C

Canal irrigation 91
Caps, use of — prohibited among Sikhs 94
Chadar 95
Chadarband 103
Chadar-dálna 97
Chamár 98, 103
Change of religion effect of — 104
Chapátis 97, 99
Characteristics of the Jat Sikhs 90
Chimta 99
China, service of Sikhs in — 93, 95
Chúhras 93, 103, 105
Chukra 94
Chúla 99
Condition of the people among the Jats 91
Cows, reverence for — 98
Crime among Sikhs 96
Customs, personal — of Sikhs 94

D

Dalán 101
Daliya 97
Daughters, value of — among Sikhs 96
Deorhi 102
Dharamsálas 91, 92, 102
Dhóti, use of — by Sikhs 95
Difference between Mánjha and Málwa Sikhs ... 91
Diwáli 105
Dólni 99
Dress of Sikhs 95

E

Education among Sikhs 92

F

Family life among Jat Sikhs 102
Females, contrast between Sikh — and Rájpútnis and Musalmánis 91
Food of the Punjáb peasant 97
Funds, village 100

PAGES.

G

CHAPTER IV—*contd.*

Gadwa 99
Gagar 99
Gháti 95
Ghi 97, 99
Gódléna 104
Granthi 102
Granth 93
Gúr 97
Gúrmukhi 92

H

Handi 99
Horse and cattle breeding among Sikhs 105
Huqah 98

I

Inheritance, laws of — 103, 104

J

Jap or Japji 95
Jats, as agriculturists 91, 103, 104
——, customs of — regarding inheritance 103, 104
——, disposition of— 91
——, influence of — on Sikh character 90
——, love of litigation of — 97
——, morality and crime among— 96
——, of the Punjáb — their principal traits 90
—— parsimonious tendencies of — 95
——, physique and military qualities of — 94
——, proverbs relating to— 91
——, social position of —... 92
——, standard of wealth among— 91
Jhatka 98
Jowár 97, 105

K

Kabbadi 94
Kachh 95
Kamin 97, 101, 103
Kangan 96
Karáhi 99
Karáparshád 98
Karehi 99
Karéwa or Karao 92, 96, 9
Khalsa 90, 92, 93

		Pages.
Chapter IV—*contd.*	Kharif	105
	Khatri	92, 103
	Kaul	99
	Kúkas	95
	Kúrta	95
	L	
	Laddu	97
	Lambardars	100
	Langar-khána	97
	Lángris...	98
	Lóta	99
	Lassi	97, 105
	Litigation	97
	M	
	Mahla	96
	Makkai	97
	Malba	102
	Mánjha and Málwa Sikhs...	91
	Mashaks...	98
	Mazbhis	93, 98
	Mélas	94
	Mirch	97
	Money-lenders	103
	Morality	96
	N	
	Nudity	94
	P	
	Pagband	104
	Pagri	96
	Pahúl	98
	Paijámas	95
	Pakhâls	98
	Pancháyats	100, 104
	Parat	99
	Parshád	98
	Patwari	100
	Pattis	100, 102
	Paucity of women	96
	Penury of Jat Sikhs	95
	Persian character, objection to use of—	92
	Physique of Jats	94
	Polyandry	96
	Post	98

		PAGES.
CHAPTER IV—*concld.*	Position, social — of Jats	92
	Prisoner's Base	94
	Proverbs of the Punjáb	91
	Púris	99
	Purification of the body	94
	R	
	Rabi	105
	Rahits, infraction of —	104
	Rájpúts	92, 94, 99, 104
	Reserve	103
	S	
	Sáfa	96
	Sahukar	103
	Salutations	95
	Sandási	99
	Sarsón	97
	Sikh women	99, 100
	—— villages	100
	Sikhism, value of — in raising the lowest classes	93
	Sirpanch	104
	T	
	Tahsildar	100
	Táwa	99
	Tháli	99
	Thúla	100, 101
	Til	97
	V	
	Villages	100
	Z	
	Zaildars	100
	Zamindars	100, 102
CHAPTER V.	Recruiting	106—112
	A	
	Ajnala	107
	Amritsar	107, 109

PAGES.

B

CHAPTER V—*contd.* Bári Doáb 106
Batala 107
Beas 106
British Officers, employment of—on recruiting duty ... 112

C

Chaj Doáb 106
Chenáb... 106
Chúnián 106
Civil authorities 109

D

Dhóti, use of—by Singhs 111
Disposal of recruits 109
Doáb 106

F

Fairs 111
Ferozepur 106

G

Gót of recruits 111
Gujrat 107
Gujránwala 106
Gurdaspur 107

H

Hoshiarpur 106, 107

J

Jhind 106
Jullundur 106
Jullundur Doáb 106

K

Kamboh 111
Kapúrthála 106
Kara, use of —by Singhs... 111
Kasur 106
Khes... 111

L

Lambardars 109
Leave and furlough men, employment of—for recruiting ... 112
Ludhiána 106

		Pages
	M	
Chapter V—*contd.*	Málwa	106
	Maler Kótla	106
	Manjah	106
	Medical inspection of recruits	109
	Múhin	111
	Múnna Sikhs...	111
	N	
	Nabha	106
	Nakódar	106
	P	
	Patiála	106
	Patti or Muhin of Sikh recruits	111
	Pay of recruits	110
	R	
	Rávi	106
	Rechna Doáb	106, 107
	Recruiting Staff	107
	——— at fairs	111
	———, method of work	108
	——— parties, composition of—	108
	———, season for—	110
	Recruits, disposal of—	109, 110
	———, pay of—	110
	———, system of obtaining	107
	———, verification of—	110
	Recruiters, rewards for—	109
	Regulations regarding recruiting	112
	S	
	Seasons for recruiting	110
	Siálkót	107
	Singhs, characteristics of—	111
	Sub-montane districts, value of—for recruiting ...	107
	Sutlej	106
	T	
	Tahsils	108
	Tahsildars and Thánadars	109
	Taran Taran	106
	V	
	Verification of recruits	110
Appendix A.—	List of districts and tahsils with their relative value as Sikh recruiting grounds and the names of some of the principal tribes found therein.	
Appendix B.—	List of principal fairs held in the Sikh Recruiting District mentioned by the Recruiting Staff officer as affording good opportunities for recruiting.	

SIKHS.

CHAPTER I.

HISTORY AND ORIGIN.

Before commencing an account of the Sikhs, it is necessary to emphasize the fact that 'Sikh' is the name given to the members of a military order of Hindu dissenters and puritans, and not, as is sometimes supposed, to any particular race. Owing, however, to the social and political preponderance of the Jats throughout the Punjáb, and to the fact that considerably more than two-thirds of the Sikh population belong to this tribe, the history of Sikhism must necessarily be prefaced by an account of the Jats, and of the circumstances which caused this race of peaceful cultivators to be transformed into a fraternity of warriors.

Disputed origin of the Jats.

Perhaps no question connected with Indian ethnology has been more frequently discussed than that of the origin of the Jats. According to some authorities they are Aryans, of the same stock as the Rájpúts, and the name of their race is simply the modern Hindi for *Yádu* or *Jádu*, the title of the famous Kshatriya clan to which the demi-god Krishna belonged. Others maintain that they are Indo-Scythians, identify them with the *Jatii* and *Getæ* or Goths of the classical geographers, and even go so far as to assert that they are of the same race as the Magyars* and Gypsies of Eastern Europe. "It may be that the original Rájpút and original Jat entered India at different periods in its history, but if they do represent two separate waves of immigration, it is at least exceedingly probable, both from their almost identical physique and facial character, and from the close communion which has always existed between them, that they belong to one and the same ethnic stock. It is, moreover, almost certain that the joint Jat-Rájpút race contains not a few tribes of aboriginal descent though it is in the main Aryo-Scythian."†

The races of ancient India.

The dawn of Indian history discloses two races struggling for the soil. One was a fair-complexioned Sanskrit-speaking people of Aryan lineage, who entered the country from the north-west; the other a dark-skinned race of lower type,

* "The strange resemblance of the Magyars to the Jats has led many ethnologists to believe that the two races are identical: not only are they alike in build, physiognomy, and warlike habits, but they brush their beards in the same fashion, and these little customs often endure longer than either manners or religion itself. It may be doubted whether Sikhs, Afghâns, Persians, Jews, Scythians, and Magyars were not all originally of one stock."—Notes on Sikhs,—*Crowther.*

† Punjab Census Report of 1881.—*Densil Ibbetson.*

the original inhabitants of the land, who were either driven by the Aryans into the hills, or reduced by them to servitude in the plains.

The cradle of the Aryan races.

The original home of the Aryan race is said to have been on the banks of the Oxus in Central Asia.* From there it migrated in two directions—one branch moved north-west towards Europe, the other south-east towards Persia and India. It is with the latter that we are here concerned.

Crossing the Hindu Kúsh, the Aryans settled for some time in the valleys of Afghánistán; from thence they forced their way across the mountains into India, and gradually settled in the Punjáb about 2000 B.C.

Early conditions of life among the Aryans.

We know very little of their manner of life. They roamed from one river valley to another with their cattle, making long halts in favourable situations to raise the crops required for their food. They were constantly at war, not only with the aboriginal tribes, but also among themselves. At the head of each tribe was a chief or *Máhárájá*, but each house-father was a warrior, husbandman, and priest, offering up sacrifices to the gods direct, without the intervention of a professional priesthood.

The Védas.

The earliest records of the Aryans are contained in the *Védas*,—a series of hymns composed in the Sanskrit language from the 15th to the 10th century B. C. by the *Rishis*, an order of devout sages, devoted to religious meditation, whose utterances were supposed to be inspired. The early *Védas* must have been composed while the Aryan tribes were marching towards India; others after their arrival on the banks of the Indus. During this advance the race progressed from a loose confederacy of various tribes into several well-knit nations, and extended its settlements from the Himalayas in the north to the Vindhyas in the south, and throughout the whole of the river systems of Upper India, as far to the east as the Sône.

Origin of the Brahmans or Aryan priests.

It has been explained that each head of a family conducted his own religious rites, but in course of time many ceremonial observances were added to the primitive religion, necessitating the service of a special priesthood. It became the custom to call upon the *Rishis* to conduct the great sacrifices and to chant the *Védic* hymns. The art of writing was at this time unknown, and hymns and sacrificial phrases had to be handed down by word of mouth, from father to son. It thus came about that certain families became the hereditary owners of the liturgies required at the great national festivals and were called upon time after time to chant the tribal battle hymns, to

*Some authorities now dispute this statement, and declare that the Aryans came from Central Europe.

invoke the divine aid, and to appease the divine wrath. These potent prayers were called *Brahmas,* and those who offered them were *Bráhmans.* By degrees the number of ministrants required for a great sacrifice increased. Besides the high priests who superintended the ceremonies, there were the celebrants who dressed the altars, slew the victims, and poured out libations to the gods, while others chanted the *Védic* hymns and repeated the phrases appropriate to particular rites. In this manner there arose a special priesthood—a class which was entrusted with the conduct of religious offices, while the rest of the community carried on their ordinary avocations of war, trade, and agriculture.

As the Aryan colonists spread east and south, subduing the aboriginal races, they were to a large extent relieved from the burden of agricultural labour through the compulsory employment of the conquered people. In this manner there grew up a class of warriors freed from the toil of husbandry, who attended the *Máharája,* and were always ready for battle. These kinsmen and companions of the kings gradually formed themselves into a separate class, and were referred to as *Kshatriyas, i.e.,* 'those connected with the royal power,' and eventually as *Rájpúts*, or 'those of royal descent.'

Origin of the warrior class.

The incessant fighting which had formed the common lot of the Aryans on their march eastward from the Indus, gradually ceased as the aboriginal races were subdued. Members of the community who from family ties, or from personal inclination, preferred war to the peaceful monotony of village-life, had to seek for adventure in the hills and forests of the lower Himalayas, or the unknown country to the south of the Vindhyas. Distant expeditions were chiefly undertaken by those to whom war was a profession, while others, more peacefully inclined, stayed at home, devoting themselves to agriculture and the manufacturing arts.

Origin of the agricultural and trading classes.

Thus the Aryans and their retainers, by a process of natural selection gradually resolved themselves into four classes :—

1. The *Bráhman* or priestly caste* composed of the *Rishis,* their descendants and disciples, to which was entrusted the expounding of the *Védas* and the conduct of religious ceremonies.

The organisation into four classes.

* The term 'caste' is derived from the Portuguese *casta,* 'a family,' but before the word came to be extensively used in European languages, it had for some time been identified with the Bráhmanic division of Hindu society into classes. The corresponding Sanskrit word is *várna* 'colour.' The three Aryan *várnas* or castes were of light complexion. Bráhmans were said to be *white,* Kshatriyas *ruddy*, and Vaisiyas *yellow:* on the other hand, the Súdras and Dasyus or aborigines are described in the *Védas* as *black.*

2. The *Kshatriya*,* *i.e.*, *Rájpút* or governing and military caste composed of the *Máharájas* and their warrior kinsmen and companions, whose duty it was to rule, fight, administer justice, and protect the community in general. It is now represented by the Rájpút and the Khatri.

3. The *Vaisiya* or trading and agricultural caste, which, assisted by the conquered aborigines, tilled the land, raised cattle, and manufactured the arms, implements, and household utensils, required by the Aryan commonwealths. It is now represented by the Banya.

4. Besides the three Aryan castes, but immeasurably beneath them, there was the servile or *Súdra* caste, composed of captured aborigines whose lives had been spared, and of the progeny of marriages between Aryans of different castes and of Aryans and the women of the country, all of which, by the rigid exclusiveness of caste custom, came to be regarded as degraded.

It must be remembered, however, that in the early days of the Aryan settlements the line of separation between the three first-named classes was far from being sharply defined. The transfer of individuals and their families from one to the other was not an uncommon occurrence, and numerous instances are recorded of kings and warriors terminating their careers as *Rishis* or saintly ascetics. Moreover, in very early times, the *Máharájas* often combined the offices of the priesthood with kingly power, a custom which in rare instances has survived to the present day. In the same way it was not unusual for the more adventurous Vaisiyas to abandon agriculture, and join the ranks of the Kshatriyas. In course of time these occupational distinctions developed into separate castes, and as intermarriage became first of all restricted, and afterwards prohibited, each caste devoted itself more strictly to its own hereditary employment. All, however, were recognized as belonging to the twice-born† or Aryan race, all were permitted to attend the great national sacrifices, and all worshipped the same gods.

But it must not be supposed, that Bráhman supremacy was accepted without protest. Their claims to recognition as a distinct Levite class, of

---

* Generally pronounced *Chhatriya* or *Chhatri*. The Rájpúts of Oudh and the North-West Provinces usually call themselves *Thákúrs*; those of Rájpútána and the Punjáb *Rájpúts*. The *Khatris* of the Punjáb, many of whom are Sikhs, profess to be a branch of the old *Kshatriya* stock which abandoned war for trade, in order to escape the wrath of Paráshu Ráma, an incarnation of Vishnu, and the champion of oppressed Bráhmans.

† The twice-born castes are the Bráhmans, the Kshatriyas or Rájpúts, and the Vaisiyas. The Súdras are excluded from this category.

divine origin, and possessed of supernatural powers, were rejected by the Kshatriyas, who insisted, with perfect truth, that many of the *Rishis* who had composed the *Védas* were kings and warriors rather than priests, and that no authority for the pretensions of the Bráhmans could be found in the *Védic* legends.

Resistance of the Kshatriyas to the pretensions of the Bráhmans.

There are traditions of a great struggle having taken place between the Bráhmans and the Kshatriyas, in which the former were completely victorious. The details of this quarrel, however, are obscure, for the Bráhmans, as exclusive custodians of the sacred writings, took care to efface all reference to a struggle which, from its very existence, cast a doubt on their pretensions to a divine origin. It may here be noticed that many of the Aryan tribes rejected the theory of Bráhmanical supremacy. Thus the earlier settlements west of the Indus never adopted the principle of caste; those between the Indus and the Jumna accepted it, but in a modified form; it was chiefly in the tract watered by the Jumna and the Ganges, from Delhi on the west to Ajudhya and Benares on the east, that the Bráhmans consolidated their authority, and became a compact, learned, and influential body, the authors of Sanskrit literature, and the lawgivers, scientists, and philosophers, of the whole of the Hindu world.

The principle of caste not of universal acceptation.

By the 5th century B. C. the original simplicity of the *Védic* worship had been replaced by a philosophical creed, accompanied by an elaborate ritual. The early conception of a Supreme Being, made manifest through the physical forces of Nature, gave way to the mystic triad of Bráhma, Vishnu, and Siva, the Maker, Preserver, and Destroyer, with a tendency to create new gods, to worship the elements in various personifications, and to embody the attributes of each member of the Hindu Trinity in numerous *avatars* or incarnations. The new religion puzzled the people without satisfying them, while the growing arrogance of the Bráhmans caused a universal desire for a return to more primitive beliefs.

The change from Védism to Bráhmánism.

At this juncture, Sakya Múni, a Kshatriya prince of Behar, initiated the great reformation which eventually developed into a new religion. Universal charity, liberty, and equality, with the total rejection of caste, formed the fundamental principles of the new doctrine, and the personal character of Buddha, the 'Enlightened,' as he was named by his disciples, immediately attracted a considerable following.

The Buddhist reformation.

The growth of Buddhism was very rapid. By about 200 B.C. it had become the state religion in Hindustán. From thence it spread north into Nepal, and through Central Asia into China and Japan. At the same time Buddhist missionaries carried their faith into Ceylon, and from thence it was extended to Burma, Siam and Java. But though Bráhmanism was undoubtedly modified by Buddhism, it was never displaced. Even in the 6th century Buddhism had commenced to decline, and before the Muhammadan faith had come fairly upon the scene, it had entirely disappeared from India. For more than a thousand years the two religions had existed side by side, and modern Hinduism is undoubtedly a combination of both.

The vitality of Bráhmanism and the decline of Buddhism.

About 400 B.C., the Bráhmans, finding in Buddhism a religious movement which threatened their spiritual authority, designed a code which, besides maintaining their privileges, formed a definite authority on all points connected with Hindu law and ritual. This celebrated work, called the Code of Mánu, and known also as the *Dharma-Shástras*, is a compilation of the customary law current about the 5th century B.C. in the Aryan principalities on the banks of the Ganges and Jumna. The Bráhmans claimed for it a divine origin, and ascribed it to Mánu, the first Aryan man. In it the fourfold division of society is said to have been ordered by Bráhma, the Creator of the Universe. The Bráhmans are supposed to have emanated from his head, the Kshatriyas from his arms, the Vaisiyas from his thighs, and the Súdras from his feet. The code consists of a mass of precepts, religious and secular, rules for the administration of justice, and special enactments with regard to purification and penance. It was written with a view to stemming the tide of Buddhist reform by stringent rules against the intermingling of castes by marriage, and by forbidding the higher castes under severe penalties from eating, drinking, or holding social intercourse with any of those ranking beneath them.

The Dharma-Shástras or Institutes of Mánu.

The reaction in favour of Bráhmanism began to have effect about 200 B.C. By the 8th century A. D. the Bráhmans had completely re-established their authority. The simplicity of the *Védic* faith was transformed beyond recognition. No efforts were spared to materialise religion. The gods were provided with wives. Caste was revived, no longer with the fourfold division of the Code of Mánu, but with all the complicated occupational sub-divisions which exist to the present day. In all these changes we trace the efforts of an astute priesthood to establish a popular religion. No section of the community was forgotten. The smouldering enmity of the Kshatriyas

The Bráhman revival.

was appeased by attributing a celestial origin to the ancestors of their ruling families. The Solar and Lunar races of Ajudhya and Mathura were flattered by the elevation of Ráma and Krishna, their respective heroes, to the dignity of *avatars*, or incarnations of the divine Vishnu. Scythian invaders and aboriginal races were conciliated by the adoption of their tribal divinities. Their *totem**, tree, and serpent worship, though utterly at variance with the spirit of the *Védas*, was affiliated to the orthodox beliefs, and their princes and warriors were accorded the status of Kshatriyas as an inducement to accept the principle of caste.

The assimilative character of Bráhmanism.

Buddhism, in spite of the antagonistic nature of its doctrines, was disposed of in a similar manner; and Buddha, whose whole life and teaching had been a protest against the formalism of the Bráhmans, was absorbed into the Hindu system, and, as an incarnation of Vishnu, was allotted a place in the pantheon of minor gods. Thus, step by step, by diplomacy and adaptiveness, the Bráhmans consolidated their authority, and established a religion which, having the *Védic* faith of the Aryan race as its foundation, has absorbed and assimilated a portion of each of the religious systems which it has successively displaced.

Greek, Bactrian, and Scythian invasions.

During the period embraced by the rise and fall of Buddhism, *viz.*, from 242 B. C. to 500 A. D., India was subjected to a series of foreign invasions. The Greeks of Bactria, expelled by hordes of Scythians, entered India in the second and first centuries B. C., and are said to have penetrated as far as Orissa. Meanwhile the *Medii*, *Xanthii*, *Jatii*, *Getæ* and other Scythian races, were gradually working their way from the banks of the Oxus into Southern Afghánistán, and the pastoral highlands about Quetta, whence they forced their way by the Bolán Pass, through the Sulaimán Mountains, into India, settling in the Punjáb about the beginning of the first century. It is from these Scythian immigrants that most of the Jat tribes are at any rate partly descended.

Geographical distribution of the Scythian races.

Starting from the banks of the Indus, which they occupied from Hazára to the coast of Scinde, the Scythians spread out in a fan-like shape from the Salt Range in the north, to the Aravulli Hills and the Chambal in the south, and as far to the east as the valley of the Jumna. They thus colonised the

* "The ruder races of men are found divided into tribes, each of which is usually named after some animal, vegetable, or thing, which is an object of veneration or worship to the tribe. This animal, vegetable, or thing, is the *totem* or *god* of the tribe. From the tribe being commonly named after its *totem*, the word is also frequently employed to signify merely the tribal designation."—*Chamber's Encyclopædia.*

Punjáb, Northern Rájpútána, and the western half of the Gangetic Doáb, and a considerable proportion of the inhabitants of these countries are undoubtedly of Scythian origin.

Shortly after their arrival in India. the majority of these Scythian immigrants became converts to Buddhism; in course of time, however, their religion was assimilated to that of their Aryan neighbours, and by the 10th century they had not only accepted the spiritual supremacy of the Bráhmans, but also, in a modified degree, the restrictions and distinctions of caste.

Conversion of the Scythian ancestors of the Jats to Hinduism in the 10th century.

The ancestors of the four agnicular or fire tribes of Rájpúts are generally considered to have been Scythian warriors who assisted the Bráhmans in their final struggles with the Buddhists, and were admitted into the ranks of the 'twice born' as a reward for their services to Hinduism. Some sort of story being necessary to account for their origin and rank, the ready-witted Bráhmans bestowed upon them the title of 'fireborn' to distinguish them from the original Rájpút races which claimed descent from the Sun and Moon.

As has before been noticed the distinction between Jats and Rájpúts is probably social rather than ethnic. "Those families of the Aryo-Scythian stock whom the tide of fortune raised to political importance, became Rájpúts, almost by mere virtue of their rise, and their descendants have retained the title with its privileges by observing the rules by which the higher are distinguished from the lower castes in the Hindu scale of precedence; by refusing to intermarry with families of inferior rank; and by rigidly abstaining from widow-marriage and refraining from menial and degrading occupations." Those who transgressed these rules fell from their high estate, and were reduced, some to the grade of a Jat or cultivator, others to that of a Gújar or herdsman.

The distinction between Jats and certain tribes of Rájpúts often social rather than ethnic.

One of the earliest of the Jat traditions, recorded by Tod in his "Annals of Rájásthán," gives a striking example of the vicissitudes of Rájpút families, and the origin of their connection with the Jats. About 550 A. D. the Scythian king of Ghazni invaded the Punjáb, and attacked Mansur Ráo, a *Yádu* Rájpút who was Rája of Salbahána or Lahore. The latter fled to the jungles with his heir, leaving his five other sons concealed in the house of a *Mahájan*.* Through the treachery of one of the Rája's subjects, the Ghazni king was informed of the children's hiding-place, which he

Legend of the Jats regarding their connection with the Yádu Rájpúts.

* A *Mahájan* is a banker and money-lender.

surrounded with a cordon of troops. The *Mahájan,* terrified by threats of immediate execution, gave up the young princes, who were made to assume the peasant's garb, feed with Jats or husbandmen, and marry the daughters of their father's *bhúmias* or cultivators. Thus it was that the *Yádu* princes fell from the rank of Rájpút and assumed the designation of Jat,* which has been retained ever since by their descendants. The truth of this legend is indirectly confirmed by the fact that the throwing of the discus or steel quoit, which, as an emblem of Vishnu, was the special weapon of the *Yádu,*† is still a favourite pastime among many of the Jats of the Punjáb.

This theory of a partially Rájpút origin is further supported by the fact that the Jats were at one time regarded as belonging to the thirty-six *ráj-kúlas* or royal tribes of India; and although the Rájpút and Jat races are now entirely distinct, and intermarriage between them is impossible, there is evidence to show that Rájpúts took Jatni wives as late as the fifth century, and there is no doubt that connections were frequently formed between them, though they may not always have been dignified by the name of marriage. From the earliest times the beauty and strength of the Jat and Gújar women won the admiration of the Rájpút princes, who received them into their *zánánas* as *khawás* or concubines; and it is more than probable that many Jat clans are descended from the offspring of such unions. "It is strange that many Jat tribes of this lineage concur in the same ridiculous story that their ancestress was a beautiful Jatni who, while going along with a waterpot on her head, stopped a runaway buffalo by pressing her foot on the rope tied to its neck, and did so without spilling the water. This feat of strength so pleased a Rájpút chieftain who was looking on, that he immediately placed her in his *zanáná,* and thus a new *gót* or family sprang from the connexion.‡"

Descent of many Jat clans from Rájpúts by Jat women.

But though the traditions of the Punjáb Jats in almost all cases refer to a Rájpút origin, and emigration to the Punjáb from the Dekhan or Central India, others claim direct descent from the Scythian adventurers who forced their way into India from Ghazni and the Kandahar valley. Thus the *Mán, Her,* and *Bhúlar* Jats of the Central Punjáb sometimes call themselves *Shibgotras,* because they profess to be descended from the *Jatta* or matted hair of Siva, in contradistinction to the *Kasabgotras* who are the descendants of Rájpúts by Jat women, or of Rájpúts who have lost grade by the practice of *karáo* or widow-marriage.

* The term Jat, in the Punjáb and Rájpútána, is practically synonymous with cultivator.
† The *Yádu* Rájpúts claim descent from Krishna, the eighth incarnation of Vishnu.
‡ Races of the North-West Provinces of India.—*Elliott.*

We know little or nothing of the ancient history of the Jats. As early as the 7th century the Jats of Scinde were ruled over by a Bráhman dynasty, and by the 11th century they had spread into the Punjáb proper. We first hear of them in the annals of the Muhammadan historians, who tell us that in 1024 the Jats of Scinde cut up several detachments of Mahmúd's army as he was returning across the desert to Ghazni, after the sack of Somnath in Guzerat. To punish these outrages, Mahmúd commenced operations against them in 1026.

The Jats harass Mahmúd's army in the Scinde desert in 1024.

The principal Jat settlements were then in the tract lying between the Indus and the Sutlej. "Finding that the Jat country was intersected by large rivers, Mahmúd, on reaching Mooltán, built a number of boats armed with iron spikes projecting from their prows to prevent their being boarded by the Jats who were experts in this system of warfare. In each boat he placed a party of ten archers, and men armed with naptha fire-balls to burn the Jat fleet. The Jats sent their wives, children, and effects to Sind-Ságar, and launched a flotilla of well armed vessels to meet the Ghaznians. A terrible conflict ensued, but the projecting spikes sank a number of the Jat boats, while others were set on fire. Few escaped from this scene of terror, and those who did, met with the more severe fate of captivity."* Many Jat tribes must have been taken away as captives to Ghazni, which would account for the vague traditional connection with that place which is claimed by so many of the clans.

Conflict between the Afgháns and the Jats.

The growing power of the Jats was so crippled by this disaster that we hear nothing more of them, or of their military exploits, until 1658, when they reappeared as valuable allies of Aurangzéb in the troubled times that followed the deposition of Shah Jahán. We cannot ascertain with any precision when the Jats of the Western Punjáb adopted Islám, but when Bábar invaded India in 1525, he found that in the Salt Range they had been subdued and converted by the Gakkars, and by the Áwáns, Janjúas, and other tribes of Rájpút rank which had adopted the Muhammadan religion. About the same time the Jats of Scinde were driven back from the foot of the Sulaimáns to the banks of the Indus by the advance of the Pathán and Balúch.

Conversion of the Jats of the Western Punjab to Islám in the 15th and 16th centuries.

West of the Indus and the Rávi the Jats became Musalmáns, and being a conquered people, of no political importance, were looked down upon by the Patháns, Mughals, and Moslems of Rájpút descent, who seized their

---

* Cyclopædia of India.—*Balfour.*

lands, and thus drove them to seek a living as nomads, wandering with their herds over the grazing-grounds of the western plains of the Punjáb.

The Muhammadan Jats of the Western Punjáb.

To this day, in Scinde and the Doáb of the Indus and Sutlej, 'Jat' is the usual term for a grazier or herdsman, and is applied indiscriminately to a congerie of various tribes, Jats proper, degraded Rájpúts, and mongrels of every race, who have nothing in common save their Muhammadan religion, their agricultural occupation, and their subordinate social position. In the same way the Balúchis who came into the lower frontier district as a dominant race, contemptuously included all cultivating tribes who were not Balúch, or of some race such as the Sayyad or Pathán, whom they had been accustomed to look upon as their equals, under the generic name of Jats, and the people themselves have lost the very memory of their origin. The proverbs of the Patháns and Balúchis are full of contemptuous references to the Jats or 'Hindkis' as they are perhaps more commonly called. "The Jat is such a fool that only God can take care of him." "Get round a Pathán by coaxing, but heave a clod at a Hindki." In short the Muhammadan Jat of the Indus Valley and the Salt Range is looked down upon as a member of an inferior race, and the position he the e occupies is very diff-rent from that which is held by his Sikh and Hindu brethren of the Central and Eastern Punjáb, and the Northern and Eastern portions of Rájpútána.

The Jats* of the Punjáb proper have been truly described as "the backbone of the province" by character and physique, as well as by numbers and locality. They are stalwart sturdy yeomen, of great independence, industry, and agricultural skill, and collectively form perhaps the finest peasantry in India"† It is probable that many of their ancestors came up the Sutlej valley into the Central Punjáb, from the country bordering on the mouth of the Bolán; but the great majority derive their origin from Rájpútána, which, about 800 years ago, was abandoned by their forefathers in favour of the fertile plains of the Málwa, and the latter, in fact, may now be regarded as the true home of the Jat Sikh.

The Jat Sikhs.

From the earliest times Jats have been remarkable for their rejection of the monarchical principle, and their strong partiality for self-governing commonwealths. One of the names by which they were known to the ancients was *Arashtra*, or

The republicanism of the Jats.

* "In the North-West Provinces and the eastern districts of the Punjáb, Hindu Jats are called Jats, pronounced Jāāts; in the Central Punjáb they are mostly Sikhs and are called Jăts, pronounced Juts. This is a mere dialectic difference. Punjábi always shortens the long *a* of Hindi, *e.g.*, *Kám* which becomes *Kumm*.—Races of the North-West Provinces of India.—*Elliott*.

† Ethnography of the Punjáb.—*Denzil Ibbetson*.

kingless; and the village community, an institution which from its organisation forms a typical example of the primitive agricultural commonwealth, has always been most flourishing in districts inhabited by Jats.

The Jats of Rájpútána, previous to their conquest by Rájpút fugitives from Kanouj in 1194, on the defeat of the latter by Muhammad Ghori, were divided into small republics which extended into the Central and Eastern Punjáb. One of these petty commonwealths, that of Phúl or Máharáj, survived to within recent times. It was afterwards broken up into the principalities of Patiála, Nábha, and Jhind, which are known to this day as the Phulkián States.

The rise of Jats due to Muhammadan persecutions and the weakness of the Mughal Empire.

Like the Mahrattas, the Jats owed their independence partly to the religious persecutions of the Musalmáns which drove them to revolt; partly to the internal dissensions of the latter days of the Mughal Empire which gave them a favourable opportunity of consolidating their power, and assuming a national character; and partly to religious fanaticism and an undying hatred of Muhammadans stirred up by the teachings of Govind Singh, the last and most famous of the Sikh *Gúrús.*

Origin of Sikhism.

The first *Gúrú*, or spiritual leader of the Sikhs, was a Khatri named Bába Nának, who was born at Talwandi near Lahore in 1469, and after travelling and preaching throughout a great portion of North-Western India, and paying a visit to Mecca, died at Kartarpur, near Jullundur, in 1539. He was succeeded by nine other *Gúrús*, and the dates between which each of them was the recognized head of the faith, are given in the margin.

1.	Bába Nának	... 1539.
2.	Angad	1539 to 1552.
3.	Amr Dás	1552 to 1574.
4.	Rám Dás	1574 to 1581.
5.	Arjún	1581 to 1606.
6.	Har Govind	1606 to 1645.
7.	Har Rai	1645 to 1661.
8.	Har Kishn	1661 to 1664.
9.	Tegh Bahadur	1664 to 1675.
10.	Govind Singh	1675 to 1708.

"In its origin Sikhism had much in common with Buddhism. Nának and Buddha alike revolted against a religion overladen with ceremonial and social restrictions, both rebelled against the bigotry and arrogance of a privileged priesthood, and the tendency of both was to quietism. The form, however, which each assumed, was largely influenced by his surroundings. Buddha lived in Behar, the centre of Hindu India, and among the many divinities of the Bráhmans; these he rejected as false, and as he could offer no substitutes, he denied the existence of God. Nának, on the other hand, was born in the Punjáb, which then formed the borderland between Hinduism and Islám; he was brought up under the shadow of the monotheism of Muhammad, and, like the latter, taught that there was one Almighty—the Creator and Director of the Universe. But that God was neither Allah nor Parméshwar, neither the God of the Musalmán nor of the Hindu, but the God of the Universe, of all mankind, and of all religions."

The burden of Nának's teaching was that all men are alike in the eyes of the Almighty. He rejected the authority of the Bráhmans and the virtue of their incantations and sacrifices, holding that salvation lay in repentance and in pure and righteous conduct, rather than in the pharisaical observance of a number of unintelligible rites. Like most Hindus, he believed in transmigration, but held that the successive stages were but means to purification, and that, at last, the soul, cleansed from its sin, returned to dwell with its Maker. "He did not despise or attack the Hindu or Muhammadan teachers; he held, indeed, that they too had been sent from God, but he preached a higher and purer religion, embracing all that was best in both. He declared himself a prophet, but he claimed neither direct inspiration nor miraculous powers. Nának prescribed no caste rules or ceremonial observances, and indeed condemned them as unnecessary and even harmful; but he insisted on no alteration in existing institutions, and was content to leave the doctrine of the equality of all men in the sight of God to work its own conclusion in the minds of his followers. He respected the Hindu veneration of the cow and the Muhammadan abhorrence of the hog, but recommended as a higher rule than either, total abstinence from flesh. In short, he attacked nothing, he condemned nobody; but he sought to draw men's minds from the shadow to the substance, to glorify what was highest and best in the religion of each, and was content to leave to all men, at least for a while, the outward and visible signs to which they were traditionally accustomed. Nothing in fact could have been more gentle or less aggressive than his doctrine; nothing more unlike the teaching of his great successor, Govind."*

The teaching of Nának.

The followers of Nának were, in popular parlance, called *Sikhs, i.e.,* 'learners,' or 'disciples,' and as the creed spread, this appellation became the descriptive title of the whole people; but it must be remembered that the term Sikh is a religious and not a racial designation, and that it belongs only to those who have accepted the faith of the *Khálsa.* The followers of Nának at the present time are the *Nának-Panthis* or *Sajdháris,*† who are *Sikhs* as opposed to *Singhs,* the name by which the followers of Govind-Singh, the tenth *Gúrú,* are particularly distinguished. *Nánaki* Sikhs are distinguished

Origin of the term Sikh.

* Ethnography of the Panjáb.—*Denzil Ibbetson.*

† These *Sajdháris* shave all but the scalp lock, called *bódi* or *choti,* which they retain just like ordinary Hindus. They are consequently known also as *Bódiwalas.*

by no outward sign. They are frequently *Múnna* or 'shaven,' and unlike their more orthodox brethren, are permitted to smoke tobacco.

Under Angad, the second *Gúrú*, who was named as his successor by Nának in preference to his own two sons, an intolerant and ascetic spirit sprang up among the adherents of the new tenets; and had it not been for the firmness and good sense displayed by his successor, Amr Dás, who recalled his followers to the mildness and tolerance of Nának, Sikhism would probably have degenerated into an obscure ascetic order. The fourth *Gúrú*, Rám Dás, founded Amritsar; but it was his successor Arjún who first gave the Sikhs a regular organization, and compiled in the *Adi Granth*, or Sikh scriptures, a rule of faith for his disciples. Arjún was in fact the Luther of the Sikh reformation. Like the latter, he insisted that the scriptures should be read to the people in the vulgar tongue, instead of in an extinct and classical language. Thus the *Granth*, which is a collection of the writings of Nának, supplemented by extracts from the works of contemporary saints, is recorded, not in Sanskrit like the *Védas* and *Puránas*, but in what was then the colloquial dialect of his followers.

The Adi Granth.

Besides giving Sikhism its bible, Arjún provided his followers with a common rallying point in the city of Amritsar, which he made their religious centre. He also reduced their voluntary contributions to a systematic levy, which accustomed them to discipline, and paved the way for further organization. True to the Khatri instinct, he was a keen and successful trader, and by utilizing the services and money of his disciples in mercantile transactions, gradually accumulated considerable wealth for his sect.

Selection of Amritsar as the centre of Sikhism.

Though famous as a pious devotee, Arjún was unable to wholly abstain from politics, and having become a partisan of Khúsrú, a son of the Emperor Jahángir, who was then in rebellion against his father, and in temporary possession of the Punjáb, the *Gúrú* was summoned to Delhi, where he was imprisoned with a rigour which hastened if it did not actually cause his death. With the arrest of Arjún began that Muhammadan persecution which was so mightily to change the spirit of the new faith: It was in fact the turning point in Sikh history, and the effect of the persecution became immediately apparent. Arjún was a priest and a merchant; but Har Govind his successor was a warrior and political leader. He abandoned the gentle and spiritual teaching of Nának for the use of arms and the love of adventure. He encouraged his followers to eat meat as giving them strength and daring. He substituted zeal in the cause for saintliness of life, and added a military system

Origin of the early Muhammadan persecutions.

The development of the military aspect of Sikhism.

to the civil organization which had already been established by Arjún. He was, however, rather a mercenary soldier than a religious zealot, and fought for and against the Mughals, as the prospect of gain dictated. Nevertheless, from the fact that his raids and forays were nearly always directed against Muhammadans, the *Gúrú* rapidly became popular with his down-trodden Hindu neighbours. All the oppressed, and many fugitives from justice, took refuge in the *Gúrú's* camp, which soon became a veritable cave of Adullam, and the chosen rallying point of those who loved plunder and a life of adventure. The policy of Har Govind was continued by his two successors, and under Tégh Bahádur the Sikhs degenerated into mere marauders and disturbers of the public peace. Choosing for his haunts the wild tract between Hansi and the Sutlej, the *Gúrú* is said to have formed an alliance with a Musalmán zealot named Adam Háfiz, and to have levied contributions from rich Hindus, while his confederate did the same from wealthy Muhammadans. The allies gave a ready asylum to criminals, and their power increased so rapidly as to menace the prosperity of the country. The imperial troops were sent against them, and they were at last defeated and taken prisoners. The Muhammadan saint was banished, but Tégh Bahádur, as an infidel, a robber, and a rebel, was executed by the Mughal authorities, who cruelly persecuted those of his followers who resisted conversion to Islám. Before his death, Tégh Bahádur appointed his son his successor, and, after enjoining upon him the necessity and the merit of revenge, begged that an effort might be made to rescue his body from his enemies. Three sweepers proceeded to Delhi for the purpose, and at great personal risk bore off the corpse of their master from the midst of a fanatical Muhammadan crowd. As a reward for their fidelity and devotion, they were immediately admitted into the community of the *Khálsa** by Gúrú Govind Singh, who bestowed upon them the title of *Mazbhi* or 'faithful.' It is from the descendants and converts of these Mazbhi Sikhs that our Pioneer regiments are now chiefly recruited.

The Sikhs degenerate into mere bandits.

The persecutions of Aurangzéb.

Origin of the Mazbhi Sikhs.

Govind Singh, the last and most famous of the *Gúrús*, was only fifteen years of age when his father was tortured and martyred by the Mughals. Under him, the fraternity which had sprung into existence as a quietest sect of a purely religious nature, and had become a military society of doubtful character, developed into the political organization which was to rule the greater part of Northern India, and to furnish the British armies with their

---

* The *Khálsá*, i. e., 'the community of God's Elect.'

stoutest and most worthy opponents. For some years after his father's execution, the lad lived in retirement, brooding over his personal wrongs and the persecutions of the Musalmán fanatics who were bathing the country in blood. During this period he finished his education which was far more complete than that of any of his predecessors.

The life and policy of Gúrú Govind Singh.

"It does not appear that this remarkable man, who, in intelligence, capacity, and fixity of purpose, was infinitely the superior of all his predecessors, undertook what he considered to be the mission of his life, in the formation of the scattered Sikh people into a formidable confederacy, and the destruction of the Muhammadan power in the Punjáb, until he was well advanced in manhood; certainly over thirty years of age. Till then he devoted himself to study, and preparation for his self-imposed duties. At the same time, not neglecting the accomplishments of a well born youth of his age, he became a keen sportsman, and skilled in all feats of arms. When he emerged from seclusion, he was at once accepted by the Sikhs as their natural and hereditary leader, and they were quite ready to follow him to avenge the murder of his father on their Muhammadan oppressors."* Before commencing his work, he desired to obtain the blessing of the Hindu goddess Dévi, one of whose shrines was on a hill near his home at Anandpur. After the practice of the necessary preliminary austerities, numerous and long continued, the goddess appeared, demanded a human sacrifice as the price of her protection, and informed him that the most acceptable offering would be the head of one of his sons. The mothers of the children naturally refused to surrender them to such a fate, so Govind Singh appealed to his friends, of whom it is recorded that five offered themselves as the sacrifice, and one, whose name is not given, was accepted and slain before the shrine. The goddess was pleased with the offering, and the subsequent career of Govind Singh and his violent death seem to have been foreshadowed in its bloody inauguration.

Meanwhile the soul of the Gúrú was filled with a passionate longing for revenge. He realised, however, the necessity for a larger following, and, imitating the example of his Muhammadan enemies, determined to make use of religion as a stepping stone to political power.

The political aspect of Sikhism.

Emerging from his retirement, he preached the *Khálsa*, the faith of the 'pure,' the 'elect,' and the 'liberated.' He openly attacked all distinctions of caste, and insisted on the equality of all who would join him; and resuscitating the old baptismal rite of the Sikhs, he proclaimed it as the *pahúl*, or 'gate,' by which all

* Ranjit Singh.—*Lepel Griffin.*

might enter the fraternity, while he gave to its members the *parshád* or communion as a sacrament of union in which the four* orders of Hindu society should eat from the same dish. Perceiving that great national weakness resulted from the disunion caused by caste, he proclaimed the social equality of all who were members of the *Khálsa*. The higher castes naturally murmured at these reforms, and many of them left him; but the lower orders rejoiced at the new dispensation and flocked in numbers to his standard. These he inspired with military ardour, with the hope of social freedom and national independence, and with abhorrence of the hated Muhammadan. He gave them outward signs of their faith in the unshorn hair, the short drawers, and the blue dress; he marked the military nature of their calling by the title of *Singh* or 'lion,' by the wearing of steel, and by the initiation by sprinkling of water with a two-edged dagger; and he gave them a feeling of personal superiority in their abstinence from the unclean tobacco. "His religious creed was in many respects the same as that of Nának. The God, the *Gúrú*, and the *Granth* remained unchanged. But, while Nának substituted holiness of life for vain ceremonies, Govind Singh demanded brave deeds and zealous devotion to the cause as the proof of faith; and though he retained the tolerance which his predecessor had extended to the Hindu gods and worship, he preached undying hatred against the Musalmán persecutors of his faith. Religious fervour was entirely eclipsed by military zeal, and thus, for the second time in history, a religion became a political power, and for the first time in India a nation arose, embracing all races, all classes, and all grades of society, and banded them together in face of a foreign foe."†

The Sikh baptism and communion.

Its effect in promoting social and national freedom.

The outward signs of Sikhism.

Govind Singh's next step was to adapt the Sikh scriptures to his own views. With this object he endeavoured to induce the custodians of the *Adi Granth* to permit him to make additions to the work; but the *Sodhis*, the Sikh priests, who had the guardianship of the sacred volume, and who were descendants of Gúrú Rám Dás, refused to accept the authority of the new leader. They, with their great establishments, had already become the Bráhmans of the Sikh creed, with all the unbounded spiritual pride of their prototypes; and when they understood that the object of Govind Singh was to preach the democratic doctrine of equality in a far more liberal fashion than it had been promulgated by even Nának himself, and that the lowest

* The four orders of Hindu society are the Bráhman or Priest; the Kshatriya or Warrior and Ruler; the Vaisiya or Trader and Agriculturist; and the Súdra or Menial.

† The Mahrattas and Sikhs would appear to afford the only instances of really national movements in India.—Ethnography of the Punjáb.—*Denzil Ibbetson.*

classes and even outcasts were to be admitted equally with themselves to the higher privileges of the *Khálsa*, they rose in revolt to a man. They denounced Govind Singh as an impostor, and refused to allow him to add his heteredox teaching to the sacred volume in their charge. They told him that if he was a true *Gúrú*, he should compile scriptures for himself, which he at once proceeded to do, the work being completed in 1696.

The *Granth* of Gúrú Govind Singh, commonly called the *Daswán Badshah ki Granth.*

The object of Govind in this compilation was not to overturn, or indeed modify in any important particulars the doctrine bequeathed by Nának, but to produce a work which should have on his excitable and fanatical followers the effect which he desired of launching them as a militant power against Islám, and recovering the Punjáb for the new congregation of the faithful. In this he was fairly successful, and at the head of a continually increasing band of devoted followers, he commenced his life-work of propagating the Sikh faith.

Govind Singh's struggles with the Mughal authorities.

The life of Govind Singh was spent in a series of petty wars, sometimes with the Hindu Rájpúts of the Hills, but more often with the Muhammadan governors of the Emperor. In one of these battles his two eldest sons were killed, and his followers reduced to forty. His mother, his wives, and two youngest children escaped with difficulty to Sirhind where the latter were cruelly buried alive by the Mughals. After this, Govind Singh was hard pressed by his enemies, who closely besieged him in his fort at Chamkaur. The last of his sons having fallen, and further resistance being hopeless, the *Gúrú* determined to take advantage of a dark night to make his escape with a handful of devoted followers. After many adventures, he escaped into the desert country round Bhattinda, where the imperial troops gave up the pursuit. From thence the dispirited fugitive repaired to Talwandi in Patiála, which he declared should be as sacred to the Sikhs as Benáres was and is to Hindus. This Sikh shrine is now known as the *Dam Damma*, or 'breathing place of the *Gúrú*,' a distinction which is also claimed by Bhattinda.

Govind Singh enters the service of the Mughals.

In 1707 Aurangzéb died, and his eldest son, Bahádur Shah, hastened from Kábul to secure the succession. He vanquished and overcame one of his brothers near Agra, and marching to the Dekhan, there defeated another, who soon after died of his wounds. While engaged in the last campaign, Bahádur Shah summoned Govind to his camp. The *Gúrú* obeyed, and was rewarded with a military command in the valley of the Godávery. "The Emperor probably thought that the leader of the insurrectionary Jats might be usefully employed in opposing rebellious Mahrattas, and Govind perhaps saw in the imperial service a ready way of disarming suspicion and of reorganizing his scattered followers." At any rate, whatever may have been Govind Singh's reasons for adopting a line of conduct which was certainly opposed to the tenor of his life and teaching, there is no doubt that he travelled at the head of his followers to the Dekhan, where he was assassinated by the sons of an Afghán horse-dealer whom he had slain in a fit of anger. He died in 1708 at Naderh, on the Godávery, which is still known to the Sikhs as Abchalnagar, *i.e.*, 'the town of the *Gúrú's* departure.' Naderh is also known as *Gúrdwára*, or the 'house of the *Gúrú*,' and numerous religious establishments, and a Sikh colony, testify to its importance as one of the holiest shrines of the religion of the *Khálsa*.

Death of Govind Singh.

Govind Singh did not live to see his ends accomplished, but he had roused the dormant spirit of the people. He was succeeded by his chosen disciple, a *Bairági** ascetic named Banda, who is said to have been a native of the Dekhan. After his master's death, Banda returned to the Punjáb, where he carried on a guerilla warfare against the Mughals with varying success for some years. He was at length driven to earth at his fort near Gurdaspur, where, in 1716, after a heroic resistance, he was forced to surrender to his enemies.

His successor Banda Bairagi.

A period of persecution followed, so sanguinary and so terrible, that for a whole generation nothing was heard of the Sikhs. A hundred Sikhs were put to death daily, contending among themselves for priority of martyrdom. Banda himself was torn in pieces by red-hot pincers after having been compelled to take the life of his only son. These and other cruelties are generally ascribed to Muhammadan fanaticism, but it must be remembered that the Sikhs were mostly bandits and outlaws, and that they brought punishment upon themselves by their excesses and defiance of the law. So long as they were merely a religious body, they were left unmolested; but when they began to band themselves together for political purposes, the Mughal authorities naturally took alarm, and commenced a series of repressive measures which increased in severity and eventually took the form of bitter religious persecutions.

Muhammadán persecutions.

From the death of Aurangzéb in 1707, began the gradual break up of the Mughal Empire. Provincial governors asserted their independence, and in

* The *Bairági* order is said to have been founded by a Hindu reformer named Ramanand whose influence on Sikhism will be noticed in Chapter III. *Bairágis* are worshippers of Vishnu. They allow their hair to grow long, and smear their bodies with wood ashes. Their distinctive mark is a string of brown crinked beads with the trident of Siva painted in white and red on their foreheads.—Ethnographical Handbook.—*Crooke.*

the general anarchy that followed, the Delhi sovereigns became mere puppets in the hands of a Mahratta confederacy. In 1738 India was invaded by the Persians under Nádir Shah. Nádir's* march through the Punjáb in 1739, met with no opposition to speak of; but the Sikhs who were fast reviving from the brutal treatment their fathers had undergone under Bahádur Shah, kept up a system of desultory plunder, robbing both the invaders and the people fleeing before them. Some years later, after the assassination of Nádir Shah, Ahmed Shah Abdáli, who had succeeded him as the ruler of Afghánistán, invaded the Punjáb, and advanced as far as Sirhind where he was defeated by the Mughals and forced to retire across the Indus. During his retreat the Sikhs plundered his baggage, cut off his stragglers, and took advantage of the prevailing anarchy to throw up a small fort near Amritsar. Their leader at this time was one Jussa Singh, a distiller by caste, who boldly proclaimed the birth of a new power in the state—the *Khálsa*, or army of the Sikh theocracy.

The invasion of Nadir Shah.

Between 1748 and 1761 the Punjáb was three times invaded by Ahmad Shah. In 1758 the Mahrattas, assisted by the Sikhs, drove out the Afgháns from Lahore; but returning in 1761, Ahmad Shah totally defeated them at Pánipat, after which he again retired to Kábul.

The invasions of Ahmad Shah.

For a time the Sikhs seemed to have some prospect of holding the Punjáb for themselves. The Mughals and their allies the Mahrattas had been defeated by the Afgháns, while the latter had retired once more across the Indus. The number and power of the Sikhs had also greatly increased. They had grouped themselves into associations, called *Misls*, in which a number of robber chiefs agreed, after a somewhat democratic and equal fashion, to follow the flag and fight under the orders of one powerful leader. This organization made them formidable. The several chiefs built their forts in convenient places, and gradually overran the whole plain country of the Punjáb, shutting up the Muhammadan governors in their strongholds at Sirhind and Lahore, which last city they twice seized and occupied for a short time.

The Sikh confederacies or Misls.

The years 1761-62 are memorable in the history of the Sikhs. Hardly had Ahmad Shah turned his face homeward, than the latter, collecting in great numbers, attacked the troops he had left in garrison at Sirhind. The Afgháns were hard pressed, and the capture of the place seemed certain, when Ahmad Shah,

The Sikh insurrection of 1761.

* "Nádir Shah was a celebrated Turkoman freebooter who drove the Ghilzai Afgháns out of Persia, and then, deposing his sovereign, usurped the Persian throne. After capturing Kandahar and Herat, he invaded India, sacked Delhi, and was assassinated in 1747, as he was returning home laden with untold spoil."—Races of Afghánistán.—*Bellew.*

by a series of rapid marches, returned to their assistance, and totally defeated his enemies. Some 20,000 Sikhs were killed and captured, among the latter being Ala Singh, the chief of Patiála. Ahmad Shah, who was a man of great sagacity, thinking it would be wise to conciliate his opponents after haven giving them so signal a proof of his power, embraced his prisoner and bestowed on him a dress of honour and the title of Rájá. This unwonted dignity aroused against Ala Singh the jealousy and anger of all the other chiefs, who declared that he had betrayed them, and that it was disgraceful for a Sikh to accept an honour conferred by a Muhammadan, a foreigner, and an enemy. Matters, however, were at length smoothed over, but Ala Singh was called upon to prove by his deeds that he was a true Sikh, and no servant of the Afghán.

Capture of Sirhind by the Sikhs in 1763.

The Sikhs were not cast down by their defeat, and no sooner had Ahmad Shah returned to Kábul than the confederacies, both north and south of the Sutlej, for once laid aside their feuds and jealousies, and united for another great effort against Sirhind,* a city which to them was peculiarly obnoxious, being the place where Govind Singh's children had been so cruelly martyred. Zin Khan, the Afghán governor, came out of the town to meet them, but was defeated and killed, and his troops utterly routed. The Sikhs immediately took possession of the city, which they plundered and destroyed in revenge for the sufferings inflicted on the family of their *Gúrú.*

The tribal quarrels of the Sikh Sirdars.

"Thus the Sikhs, both by their defeat and their victory, acquired a status which they did not before possess, and had they known how to put aside private jealousies and unite habitually as they had done for the conquest of Sirhind, they would have become as formidable in Northern India as the Mahrattas in the south and west. But the democratic nature of the Sikh faith, responding to the natural sentiments of the people, resisted all attempts at dictation by a central authority, until Máháràja Ranjit Singh broke down all opposition, and reduced rivals and enemies to a common obedience." The history of the Sikhs from the middle of the 18th to the beginning of the 19th century is a record of struggles for pre-eminence among the chiefs of the different *Misls* or confederacies, who fought against each other more often than against their common enemies the Muhammadans. Even within the borders of each *Misl* itself, the *Sirdars* were always quarrelling, and first one chief and then another took the lead. This was due, no doubt, to

* The town of Sirhind was cursed by Govind Singh in revenge for the murder of his children. "He ordered his followers whenever they passed it on pilgrimages to or from the Ganges to throw two bricks taken from its walls into the Sutlej or the Jumna, otherwise their bathing in the holy river would not profit them. This is still an invariable practice with the Sikhs who travel through the town on foot."—Ranjit Singh.—*Lepel Griffin.*

the constitution of Sikhism, under which no such thing as vassalage or feudal superiority was acknowledged. The principle of the creed was fraternity, and it was the boast of the Sikhs that they were communities of independent soldiers. While the *Khálsa* was still in its infancy, this idea of independence represented a state of things not far removed from the truth;

Causes which led to the rise of the great Sikh chieftains.

but as the more important chiefships gradually increased in power, their smaller neighbours were compelled, either for security against others, or to avoid absorption altogether, to place themselves under the protection of some leader able to defend them, rendering service in the field in return. "All that a Sikh chief asked from a follower in those days was a horse, a sword, and a matchlock. All that a follower sought was protection, and permission to plunder in the name of God and the Gúrú, and under the banner of his chief or *Sirdar*." All the great Sikh families owe their origin to the power of the sword. To attract followers by his power and success was the main desire of every Sikh chieftain. Who they were and what were their antecedents, were matters of no consequence, if only they could fight and ride. In those days every village became a fort. A neighbour, as with the Jews and Patháns,

Condition of society among the Sikh States.

was synonymous with an enemy, and cultivators ploughed their fields with matchlocks by their side. No man could consider his land, his horse, or his wife, secure, unless he was strong enough to defend them; for although the Sikh leaders were best pleased with the spoil of Muhammadans or the capture of an Imperial convoy, they were really more robbers than patriots, and plundered all with the frankest impartiality. "Yet, while the Sikhs were undoubted robbers, and though cattle-lifting was as honourable a profession amongst them, as it was on the Scottish Border a few hundred years ago, their enthusiasm for their faith, coupled with their hatred for Musalmáns who had so long trampled them underfoot, gave them a certain dignity, and to their objects and expeditions an almost national interest."*

Lahore was held by three Sikh chiefs, when, in 1797 and the following years, Zamán Shah, grandson of Ahmad, brought an army from Kábul, with

Invasion of Zamán Shah, 1797.

a view to recovering the Punjáb, only to be recalled on each occasion by troubles nearer home. He secured Lahore without opposition, and on leaving in 1798, made over the city to a young noble who had attracted his attention and rendered him valuable service. This was Ranjit Singh, the son of a Sikh *Sirdar* who had risen to considerable power towards the end of the 18th century. Ranjit was a man of strong will and immense energy; of no edu-

* Ranjit Singh.—*Lepel Griffin.*

cation but of great acuteness in acquiring knowledge that would be of practical use to him. He soon united all the separate confederacies of Sikhs under his own control, and thus acquired a general authority over all the Sikhs of the Punjáb. In 1808 his endeavours to include within his jurisdiction the Sikh principalities south of the Sutlej, forced the chiefs of these states to place themselves under British protection. Foiled in this direction, Ranjit Singh strengthened his authority in the Punjáb proper, and steadily extended his dominions in the west. In 1809 he obtained possession of Kángra which the Nepalese were then besieging. In 1813 he acquired the fort at Attock on the Indus; and in the same year obtained from Shah Shúja, the fugitive Amir of Kábul, what he coveted as much as territory—the celebrated Koh-i Núr diamond, which Nádir Shah had carried off as loot from Delhi. In 1818, after some failures in previous years, he captured the fortress of Mooltán. Kashmir, which had successfully opposed him on several occasions, was annexed soon afterwards, also the southern portion of the country that lay between the Indus and the hills. The Peshâwar valley was not added until some years later. The Trans-Indus districts, however, were left very much to themselves, and only received a visit when revenue had to be collected.

Rise of Máhárája Ranjit Singh.

The Sikh conquests.

The Sikh army was generally known as the *Dal Khálsa*, or 'Army of God.' It consisted for the most part of cavalry, who found their own horses, and received a double share of prize-money. Each chief, in proportion to his means, furnished horses and arms to his retainers, who were called *Bargirs;* and as the first tribute exacted from a conquered district was invariably horses, the infantry soldier was, after a successful campaign, generally transformed into a trooper. The infantry, previous to the formation of a regular army by Ranjit Singh, was considered an inferior service, and the only portion which enjoyed any consideration was that composed of *Akális*, or 'immortals,' a band of religious enthusiasts and warriors, who dressed in blue, and wore knife-edged quoits round their turbans, partly for show, and partly for use as missiles. These military devotees, excited by opium and *gánja*, were generally the first to enter a breach; but though they often rendered excellent service, their temper was lawless and uncertain and in times of peace they enjoyed almost boundless license.

The Sikh Army.

The Akális.

The series of brilliant victories won by Lord Lake over the Mahrattas, impressed the Sikhs with the value of disciplined troops. In 1805 Ranjit

Singh is said to have paid a secret visit to the British camp, and in 1809 he witnessed in the streets of Lahore the repulse of a fanatical band of *Akális* by the native infantry escort of the British envoy. This incident is said to have decided him to raise regular troops. By 1812 he had formed several battalions, drilled chiefly by men who had resigned or deserted from the East India Company's service. The majority of his troops were Sikhs, but there were several corps of Hindustánis and Gúrkhas, and the artillery was chiefly composed of Muhammadans. The transformation of the feudal levies of the *Khálsa* into regular disciplined troops was not effected without difficulty. The Sikhs disliked the rigidity and precision of the infantry drill, and it was only by offers of liberal pay, and by himself taking part in their manœuvres, that Ranjit Singh induced his subjects to submit to the European system of discipline. In spite of much opposition from the older *Sirdars*, the infantry gradually became the *corps d'elite*, and before the Máharája's death had come to be regarded as the true array of the *Khálsa*.

Formation of a regular army by Ranjit Singh.

During the Máhárája's reign, enlistment in the regular army, or *Khás Fauj*, was entirely voluntary; but there was never any difficulty in obtaining recruits, the infantry, especially, being composed of the handsomest and strongest young men. Under their trained instructors the *Khálsa* battalions became a formidable body of troops, well disciplined and steady, though perhaps rather slow in manœuvring. Their endurance, however, was remarkable, and it was not unusual for whole regiments to make 30 mile marches often for days at a time. The cavalry was constituted in much the same manner as in the early days of the *Khálsa* "when clouds of irregular horsemen hung on the skirts of the Afghán armies, afraid to venture an attack, but cutting off convoys and endangering the communications of the enemy."

Conditions of service in the Khálsa Army.

Following the example of Scindia and Holkar, Ranjit Singh, while gradually raising his army, received into his service several French and Italian officers, who organized his troops and greatly improved his artillery. They were not, however, entrusted with commands in the field, as these were generally reserved for the Sikh *Sirdars*. Of all the generals of the Máharája, Diwán Mokhan Chand, a Khatri, was perhaps the ablest. Another leader of the same class, named Diwán Chand, earned considerable distinction as the conqueror of Kashmir and Mooltán. The Murat of the *Khálsa* was Hari Singh, a leader of infinite dash and gallantry,

Employment of French and Italian officers.

who died at Jamrúd in 1836. His son, Jowáhir Singh, who inherited all his father's valour, led the splendid charge of irregular cavalry against the British at Chillianwala, which so nearly turned that doubtful battle into a defeat.

Ranjit Singh died in 1839, and was succeeded by Kharrak Singh, his eldest son, a weak and incapable prince, under whose rule the history of the Punjáb became a record of intrigues and deeds of violence. The reigns of Kharrak Singh and his son, Nao Nihál Singh, were short and uneventful. The former died by the hand of an assassin, the latter by the fall of a beam from a gateway. They were succeeded by two reputed sons of Ranjit—Sher Singh, who was murdered, and Dalip Singh, an infant, who was placed on the *masnad* through a palace intrigue.

The successors of Ranjit Singh.

Ranjit Singh had left an army of 92,000 infantry, 32,000 cavalry, and nearly 400 guns. It was a force which his feeble successors were totally unable to control. When one after another of those nominally in power had been assassinated, and the treasury plundered, the army, unpaid and unmanageable, demanded to be led into British territory. "It was," in fact, "no longer the willing instrument of an arbitrary government, but looked upon itself and was regarded by others as the representative body of the Sikh people. The soldiers were sensible of the advantages of systematic union, and were proud of their armed array as the visible body of Govind Singh's commonwealth." As a general rule the troops were obedient to their appointed officers, but the concerted action of each regiment and brigade was invariably regulated by a *panchâyat* of five representatives, chosen from each battalion in consideration of their character as Sikhs, or from their particular influence in their villages. In the crude form of representation thus achieved, the Sikh people were enabled to interfere with effect, and some degree of consistency, in the nomination and removal of their rulers. But these large assemblies sometimes added military license to the barbarous ignorance of uneducated cultivators. Their resolutions were often unstable or unwise, and the representatives of different brigades were not unfrequently bribed and cajoled by unscrupulous and ambitious ministers striving to acquire a preponderance of political power.

Usurpation of power by the Sikh army.

The regimental panchayats.

Their ignorance and venality.

The authority of the army gradually increased. In 1845, the Prime Minister Jowáhir Singh was executed by order of the regimental *panchâyats*, and the

The treachery of the Sikh Sirdars.

territorial chiefs, thoroughly alarmed, decided that the only way in which they could preserve their own authority was to remove the army by inducing it to engage in a war with the English which would probably result in its defeat and dispersion.

The history of the war is too well known to need recapitulation. The battles of Múdki, Firózshahr, and Aliwál were followed by the rout of the Sikh army at Sobráon, when they were driven back into the Sutlej with great loss, and the British army advanced to Lahore. On the 9th March 1846, a treaty was concluded with the Sikh *Darbar*, acting on behalf of the young Máharája Dalip Singh. By this treaty, the Jullundur and Kangra districts were ceded to the British. The latter further demanded a money payment of £1,500,000; but the hill country between the Beas and the Indus, including Kashmir and Hazára, was eventually accepted in lieu. The services of Guláb Singh, Rája of Jummoo, in procuring the restoration of friendly relations between the Sikhs and the British, were rewarded by the sale to him of Kashmir for 75 lakhs of rupees. At the urgent request of the *Darbar*, a British force was left at Lahore for the protection of the Máharája and the maintenance of his authority. To restore order, and introduce a settled administration, a British Resident was also appointed, who was to guide and control the Council of Regency.

The Sutlej campaign.

Peace was not long preserved. Early in 1848 the Governor of Mooltán, Diwán Múlráj, applied for permission to resign. Two British officers were sent by the Resident to relieve him, but they were treacherously murdered, their escort going over to the enemy. Meanwhile Herbert Edwardes, then in charge of the Déraját, hearing of the attack on his comrades, hastily collected some levies, and rapidly advanced to their assistance. He arrived too late, but at once attacked Mooltán, which proved, however, to be far too strong to be captured by a force of irregulars. Inaction caused the movement to spread, the field of operations widened, and before the end of the year the greater portion of the Punjáb was in a state of insurrection, and the *Khálsa* army engaged in hostilities with the British. Mooltán was taken after a lengthy siege. The hard fought battle of Chillianwala on the 13th January 1849, left the Sikhs as undaunted as they had been in the previous campaign after the two days' fighting at Firózshahr; and it needed the crushing defeat of Gújrat in 1849, like that of Sobraon in 1846, to bring the war to a conclusion.

The second Sikh war.

On the termination of the Sutlej campaign, the Government of India, impressed by the stubborn valour displayed by the Sikhs, determined to utilize for the native army the splendid fighting material which the conquest of the Punjáb

Raising of Sikh corps for the British service.

had placed at their disposal. In 1846 orders were issued for the formation of two Sikh battalions at Ferozepore and Ludhiána respectively, and ten years later another regiment was raised, for service among the Sonthâls, which soon became famous as 'Rattray's Sikhs.'* Besides these special corps, the commandants of regular regiments were directed to enlist 200 Sikhs per battalion; but the Hindustánis, of which they were then composed, disliked the introduction of strangers, and through the lax state of discipline which then prevailed, the order was only partially carried out. In 1849 the policy of giving military employment to the Sikhs was extended yet further by the formation of the Corps of Guides and a brigade of all arms, for police and general purposes on the border, both of which were largely composed of the former soldiers of the *Khálsa*, and formed the nucleus of the Punjáb Frontier Force.

The loyalty of the Punjáb secured by an able system of administration.

The annexation of the Punjáb was followed by a settlement of the land-tax at an assessment very much lower than that which had been levied by the Sikhs. Roads and canals were laid out, and a simple but equitable code of civil and criminal procedure established, thoroughly suited to the temper of the people. The security to life and property enjoyed under the new government and the enormous personal influence of such able officials as the two Lawrences, Nicholson, and Herbert Edwardes, was felt in the furthest corner of the province, and caused the Punjáb to remain quiet and loyal after only eight years' experience of English rule, while the people of the North-West Provinces, who had been British subjects for upwards of half a century, revolted almost to a man.

The Mutiny.

The story of the Mutiny is too well known to need more than a passing notice. After the escape of the Meerut mutineers to Delhi, where they placed themselves under the nominal authority of the titular Mughal Emperor, the rebellion was given a rallying point, and identified with the restoration of the Muhammadan power. In the North-West Provinces and Oudh, the revolt spread like wild-fire. The people sympathised with, and in most instances supported the insurgents, while the British troops serving in this district were too few to do much more than hold their own, and protect the women and children entrusted to their care. In the Punjáb our position was equally precarious, but certain circumstances rendered it rather more hopeful. In the first place the administration of the province was in the hands of

* These three battalions are now known as the 14th, 15th, and 45th Sikhs.

conspicuously able men, who, knowing the dangerous condition of the native army, forestalled the revolt of the sepoys by a timely and general disarmament. Owing to the recent annexation of the Punjáb, the British garrison was larger there than it was elsewhere, and, from their being scattered over a large area, the native troops were unable to act in concert; the latter, moreover, were in the midst of a hostile population which regarded them with indifference and suspicion—an indifference which was converted into absolute hatred when it became known that the avowed object of the Hindustáni sepoys was to restore the dominion of the hated Mughals. The spirit of the *Khálsa*, which had been humbled by the defeats on the Sutlej, was aroused at the thought of a combat between Sikhism and Islám. Delhi, the centre of the Sepoy Mutiny, was associated in their minds with the memory of bitter persecutions and the torture and martyrdom of their *Gúrús;* thus when urgent demands for troops caused Lawrence to raise local levies, the Sikhs flocked in numbers to our standards, and identified themselves with the British cause with a loyalty which never wavered. While the newly-raised regiments and the corps of the Frontier Force were earning fame and distinction before Delhi, their comrades of the 14th and 45th Sikhs were rendering splendid service in Oudh and the North-West Provinces. The former, besides saving the fort at Allahabad from falling into the hands of the rebels, took a distinguished part in Havelock's advance on Lucknow, and in the subsequent defence of the Residency. The latter, rejecting the numerous efforts made to seduce them from their allegiance, took a prominent share in the suppression of the Mutiny in Behar, and gained special distinction by the gallantry of a small detachment in defending a house at Arrah against the Dinapore mutineers.

The disarmament of the sepoys.

The Sikh revival.

The services of the Sikhs in the Mutiny.

The reorganization of the Bengal Army which followed the Mutiny, led to a complete change in its class constitution. The Hindustánis of the regiments which had either revolted or been disbanded, were replaced by the Sikhs, Dogras, Punjábis, and Patháns, of the levies raised by Lord Lawrence, and the history of India during the last forty years bears ample testimony to the military qualities of these races. It would be difficult indeed to select a more striking example of military constancy and devotion than that given by the heroic band of Sikhs who defended Saraghiri. True to the martial instincts of their faith, they died to a man at their posts, covering themselves with glory, and giving imperishable renown to the grand regiment to which it was their privilege to belong.

Reorganization of the Bengal Army.

CHAPTER II.

CLASSIFICATION AND GEOGRAPHICAL DISTRIBUTION.

The Sikh recruiting-ground extends from the Indus on the west to the Jumna in the east, and from the Bikaneer desert in the south to the lower ranges of the Himalayas in the north. It thus includes the whole of the Punjáb plains, except the country lying between the hills and the Indus, Baháwalpur, and those districts bordering on Rájpútána and the Jumna which before the Mutiny were known as the Delhi Territories. This vast tract is generally divided for purposes of recruiting into two areas, called the Mánjha and the Málwa respectively, details of which will be found in Chapter V.

The limits of the Sikh recruiting ground.

The Mánjha, strictly speaking, is the name given to the southern portion of the Bári Doáb, or country lying between the Beás and the Rávi in the neighbourhood of Lahore and Amritsar. But by a convenient enlargement of the term it may now be held that a Mánjha Sikh is a Sikh recruited from any of the districts north of the Sutlej.* The Málwa, on the other hand, is the country immediately south of the river, which stretches towards Rájpútána and the Jumna. It must not be confused with the Málwa of the Dekhan,—a rich country north of the Nerbudda, the centre of which is Indore. The ancestors of the Málwa Jats were mostly Hindu peasants, who, about the middle of the 16th century, emigrated from Jeysalmeer and settled in the Central Punjáb as peaceful subjects of the Muhammadan Emperors. The term Málwa, however, is now used in a far more extended sense, and it may be accepted as a rough rule, that a Málwa Sikh is any Sikh belonging to a district lying to the south of the Sutlej. Though essentially of the same race, the two classes are distinguished from one another by certain well-known distinctions of speech and dress, and a slight but mutual antipathy.

The difference between a Málwa and a Mánjha Sikh.

As regards military qualities, it is doubtful whether there is anything to choose between the two. "The Mánjha Sikh is as a rule brighter, smarter, quicker, and more refined than the Málwai, while the latter on the other hand is more stubborn, works quite as conscientiously but less cheerfully,

* It may be mentioned, however, that the Sikhs of the country between the Beás and the Sutlej, *i.e.*, Kapurthala, Jullundur, and Hoshiarpur, are generally called Doába Sikhs. Their lands are fertile, and they as a rule prefer agriculture to soldiering. This, coupled with he fact that their Sikhism is rather lax, renders them, in the opinion of some commanding officers, somewhat inferior as soldiers to the men of the Málwa and the Mánjha.

and from his very stolidity and obtuseness is equally staunch, while nowise inferior in either courage or discipline."

The races that embrace Sikhism.

Sikhism, like Islám, being a religion open to all classes, includes amongst its adherents members of many races and castes. Of these by far the most important and numerous are the Jats; but no account of the Sikhs would be complete without some notice of the Bráhmans, Rájpúts, Khatris, Arόras Labánas, Mahtons, Sainis, Kambohs, Kalàls, Tarkháns, Nais, Chhimbas, Jhinwars, Rámdásias, and Mazbhis, all of whom are represented in the great military brotherhood of the *Khálsa.*

JAT SIKHS.

The Jat Sikhs are divided into numerous clans, of which the following are the most important:—

Bhular.	Bat or Bath.	Gharéwál.	Khang.	Sánsi.
Mán.	Chahil or Chahal.	Gil.	Khosa.	Sidhu.
Hér or Puréwál.	Chaman.	Gorâya.	Pannun.	Sindhu or Sandhu.
Aulak.	Chima.	Hinjra.	Randháwa.	Tarár.
Bains.	Déo.	Hundal.	Sahi.	Varaich or Chung.
Bajwa or Bajju.	Dhaliwál or Dhári-wál.	Uthwal.	Sahóti.	Virk.
Bal.	Dhillon.	Khaire.	Sohal.	...

The total Jat population according to the last census was over four millions, of which a little over a million were Sikhs. For a complete list of all Jat clans, Part III of the Punjab Census Report of 1892 may be consulted.

In the following notes, the number placed before the name of each clan is the index by which its approximate geographical distribution may be traced on the map.

1. *Bhular, Mán, and Hér.*—These three Jat tribes disclaim a Rájpút origin and say they are *asl* or 'true' Jats sprung from the *Jatta* or matted hair of Siva. Claiming a common descent, they do not intermarry. The tribal divinity or *Jathera* of the *Bhular* is an ancestor named Yar Pir Bhurawala, who earned the distinction by turning a blanket into a sheep. Members of this clan will not wear, sit, or sleep on a striped blanket. The *Bhular* are found mostly in the Lahore and Ferozepore districts, but the *Mán* and *Hér* are widely distributed. The popular fable regarding their origin is that Siva was married to Parbatti, the daughter of Rája Dashpat. The latter took a dislike to his son-in-law, and declined to invite him to his *darbar*. Parbatti was so incensed at the slight put upon her

husband that she threw herself into a furnace and was consumed. On hearing of this calamity, Siva's feelings got the better of him. He unravelled his *Jatta* or coil of matted hair and with it smote the ground. From this contact sprang the ancestor of the *Bhular*. He then tore open his breast and a child came forth from whom the *Mán* are descended. Finally from his navel, which he proceeded to claw open, was produced a child of very diminutive stature who was the progenitor of the *Hér*. From his small size the *Puréwál* or *Hér* have come to be known as equal to one-half only of the tribes of *Mán* and *Bhular* which together number about 45,000 Sikhs. The *Mán* clan is famous throughout the Punjáb for valour and fidelity.

2. The *Aulak* claim descent from the solar race of Rájpúts and say their ancestor was one Aulak, who lived in the Mánjha. The *Aulak* are related to the *Sekhu, Sohal*, and *Déo* tribes with which they do not intermarry. They are found chiefly in Amritsar and muster about 10,000 Sikhs.

3. The *Bains* are found chiefly in Hoshiarpur and Jullundur. They say they were originally *Janjua* Rájpúts and that their ancestor came into Eastern Doáb in the time of Firózshah. They maintain, the tradition of their Rájpút origin by not practising *karewa* or widow-marriage, and by wearing the *janéo*, or sacred thread, at weddings. They enlist freely and make excellent soldiers.

4. The *Bajwa* or *Bajju* Jats are mostly settled in Sialkót. They claim to have been originally Solar* Rájpúts, and relate that their ancestor, Raja Shalip, was driven out of Mooltán in the time of Sikandar Lodi. Shalip had two sons,—Kals and Les. Kals, who was also known as Bajwa, escaped in the guise of a falconer and married into a Jat tribe. The Rájputs disowned the family, who then sank to the social level of their maternal relatives. The name of the tribe is derived from *Baj*, a corruption of *Baz*, 'a hawk,' in allusion to the disguise adopted by their ancestor. The *Bajwa* practice *Jandian* (see Chapter III) and are said to intermarry amongst themselves.

5. The *Bal* are probably descended from the *Bal* Rájpúts of the Malwa. They are related to the *Sekhu* tribe with which they do not intermarry. The *Bal* have a hereditary feud with the *Dhillon* with whom they will neither eat, drink, nor intermarry. They are found chiefly in the Mánjha and Doába districts.

6. The *Bát* or *Báth*.—This clan claims as its ancestor a *Súrajbansi* Rájpút named Sain Pál, who emigrated from the Málwa district about 800 years ago and settled in Lahore and Amritsar. Sain Pál is said to have had 21 sons, who each became founders of separate septs.

* Rájpúts claim to be descended either from the sun, or the moon, or from *Agni*, *i.e.*, fire. They are thus classified as Solar, Lunar, or Agnicular Rájpúts.

7. The *Chahal* or *Chahil* form a large clan of about 30,000 Sikhs, which is most numerous in Patiála, but is found also in Umballa, Ludhiána Amritsar, Sialkót and Gurdaspur. The tribal tradition is that a *Súrajbansi* Rájpút named Agarsén had four sons,—Chahil, China, Chima and Sahi,—and that the four Jat tribes bearing those names are their descendants. The *Chahil* probably emigrated into the Málwa district from Northern Rájpútána about the time of the Emperor Akbar.

8. The *Chaman* tribe claims to be descended from Rájpúts of the Lunar race. They are found chiefly in Sialkót, and have some very curious marriage customs entirely different to those of other Jats. "After tying a thread round the bridegroom's wrist, a square is drawn in a corner of the house, in which is placed an idol of grass which they worship. On a Monday, six or seven days before the marriage, cakes are distributed, seven to each married man, and four to each bachelor. Seven pitchers are filled with water, and coloured cloths tied over the mouths of the party. The water is then poured over the head of a goat, and when he shakes himself they imagine that their ancestors are pleased."

9. The *Chima* is one of the largest and most powerful Jat tribes of the Punjáb, but comparatively few are Sikhs. They claim to be descended from agnicular or 'fireborn' Rájpúts through their ancestor Chima, who was a *Chauhán* related to the Hindu Rájas of Delhi. They are most numerous in Sialkót and Gujránwála. They intermarry with all other Jat tribes, and employ *Jógis* instead of Bráhmans as their household priests. The clan has the reputation of being rather quarrelsome with its neighbours. There is a branch of the *Chima* known as *Magara*. The *China* clan is quite distinct from, though often confused with, the *Chima*. It is found in the Amritsar, Lahore, Gurdaspur, and Sialkót districts.

10. The *Déo* clan claims a very ancient origin, but there are grounds for believing that like the *Bhular*, *Mán*, and *Hér*, they are of *asl* or non-Rájpút origin. Their *Jathera* or ancestor worship is carried out with peculiar rites. The shrines are always close to a pool or tank, and as the men come out of the water their foreheads are marked by a Bráhman with a drop of blood taken from a goat's ear. The *Déos* are found chiefly in the Sialkót district.

11. The *Dhaliwal*, *Dhaniwal*, or *Dhariwal* clan claims to be connected with the *Bhátti* Rájpúts. It is found chiefly in Ludhiána, Ferozepore, and Patiála, but the non-Sikh portion of the clan extends into the Delhi Territories, Rájpútána, and the Jumna Valley. The Rána of Dhólpur is a *Dhaliwal* Jat. The tribe has a curious tradition, which is shared by

many other clans of Jats and Gújars, that a daughter of one of their headmen was married to the Emperor Akbar under the following romantic circumstances. One day a Jatni damsel was standing near the village well with two *ghurrahs* of water on her head, when a young buffalo, that had escaped from its owner, rushed passed her, trailing a cord attached to its neck. By simply placing her foot on the rope, the sturdy maiden captured the runaway without so much as losing her balance. The Emperor, who was watching, was so pleased with this feat, that he made immediate proposals of marriage, as he felt sure that a woman gifted with so much strength and courage, would be the mother of equally valiant and determined sons. The father, however, would not consent to the match without the leave of his fellow-castemen. A *panchâyat*, consisting of 35 Jat and Rájpút *lambardars*, was accordingly assembled to consider the proposal. The former raised no objections to the marriage, the latter held that it would be disgraceful. The Jats, in recognition of their friendly feeling, were rewarded by Akbar with large grants of land, and their descendants are still honourably known as '*the painti*,' or 'thirty-five.' The clan numbers about 50,000 Sikhs, and has only 2 *muhins*.

12. The *Dhillon* profess to be descended from Lunar Rájpúts settled in Hissar. They do not intermarry with the *Gorâya*, as the two clans are said to be distantly related. Their hereditary enemies are the *Bal*, with whom they will neither eat nor drink. Dhillon, the founder of the clan, was the grandson of a Rája named Karan, whose charity was such that he is said to have bestowed thirty seers of gold as alms before partaking of his daily food. The clan has a high reputation for good faith, musters nearly 50,000 Sikhs, and is found throughout the Punjáb, but more especially in Amritsar and Gujránwála. The *Dhillon* practice *jathéra*, their ancestral divinity being Gaggúwána. They are said to have 70 *muhins*.

13. The *Gharéwál* assert that they are the descendants of a Rájpút worthy named Rája Kikh, whose son, Bairsi, settled in Ludhiána and married a Jatni. From this marriage there was issue one son, Gharé, who gave his name to the tribe. The *Gharéwál* hold a high position among other Jat tribes and are sometimes called *sahú lóg* or 'superior people.' They are proud and poor, and much prefer military service to agriculture. Their physique is excellent, and they always make first rate soldiers. Contrary to the usual practice among Jats, the *Gharéwál* seclude their women. They worship an ancestor named Bába Alla, and practise *jathéra* rites by taking a little blood from a goat's ear and smearing it on the tip of the little finger of the right hand. Water is then placed in the goat's mouth, and when he gurgles, the omen is regarded as propitious.

14. The *Gil* is one of the largest and more important of the Jat tribes. Their headquarters are in Lahore and Ferozepore, but they are found all along the Beás and Upper Sutlej, and under the hills as far to the west as Sialkót. Gil, their ancestor, was a Jat of *Raghúbansi* Rájpút descent, who settled in Ferozepore and claimed to be descended from Pirthi Pál, Rája of Mithila or Behar, and a *Waria* Rájpút by a *Bhútar* Jatni wife. The following tradition explains the origin of *gil*, the tribal name, which means 'moisture.' The Rája had no children by his Rájpútni wives, but the Jatni bore him a son. The former, through jealousy, exposed the infant in a marshy spot, where he was found by the Rája's *múnshi* and called Gil, from the damp nature of the place in which he was discovered.

The *Gil* of the Ferozepore district have been described as the steadiest and most prosperous of cultivators, possessing in an eminent degree the military qualities which distinguish the Málwa Jat. The tribe is divided into 12 *muhins* known as *Asl-Gil, Gil-Gil, Sher-Gil, Vairsi-Gil, Wadan-Gil, Sudr-Gil, Kalingar-Gil, Nijjar-Gil, Jhulli-Gil*, etc. About 100,000 of the *Gil* Jats are Sikhs.

15. The *Góráya* claim descent from a *Chandrabansi* Rájpút of the same name whose grandson Mal emigrated into Gújránwála from Hissar. They are probably of the same stock as the *Dhillon* with whom they do not intermarry. They are most numerous in Gújránwála, Sialkót, and Gurdaspur. Only a few, who belong chiefly to the *Ghumman* subdivision, are Sikhs, the majority being now Musalmáns.

16. The *Hinjra*, like the *Goráya*, claim to be of *Chandrabansi* Rájpút origin, and were originally inhabitants of Hissar. They are Gújar herdsmen rather than Jat agriculturists, and are found chiefly in Gújránwála and Sialkót.

17. The *Hundal* and *Uthwal* are small tribes of *Súrajbansi* Rájpút descent, found in Amritsar, Ludhiána, Jullundur and Patiála. The latter say that their ancestor, Máharáj, received the nickname of *Unthwál* from his love of camel-riding. Only a few are Sikhs.

18. The *Khaire* profess to be the descendants of a Rájpút named Sain Pál, whose 21 sons founded 21 separate clans. The tribe worships two ancestors, one named Ráj Pál, and the other his grandson Shahzáda, who was killed in a quarrel with his neighbours the *Khangs*, with whom the *Khaire* will not intermarry. The *Khaire* are found chiefly in Amritsar.

19. The *Khang* profess to be of *Raghúbansi* Rájpút origin and state that their ancestors were originally settled near Delhi. This story, however, is at variance with another tradition which makes them out to have emigrated from Ghazni, unless, as has been suggested, they are the descendants of

a band of captives carried off to Ghazni by one of the early Muhammadan invaders of India. The *Khang* are most numerous in the neighbourhood of Sialkót and Amritsar. The tribal divinity is an ancestor named Baba Malla, who was killed in a fray with the *Khaire* Jats about the time of Akbar, and who is said to have distinguished himself by going on fighting after his head had been severed from his body.

20. The *Khosa* and *Malhi* are small tribes of Rájpút origin belonging to the Lahore district.

21. The *Pannún* claim a Rájpút origin, but like the *Khang* have a traditional connection with Ghazni. They muster about 9,000 Sikhs, and are found chiefly round Amritsar.

22. The *Randháwa* are a widely distributed tribe claiming as their ancestor a celebrated Rájpút warrior called Randháwa whose name is said to signify martial prowess.* The descendants of this worthy who now number about 25,000 Sikhs, left their home in Bikaneer about 700 years ago, and settled in Amritsar and Gurdaspur.

23. The *Sahi* clan is found chiefly in Siálkót. The tribal tradition is that their ancestor was a *Súrajbansi* Rájpút, who after being carried off by Mahmúd to Ghazni, returned to India and settled with his family on the banks of the Rávi.

24. The *Sahóti* are widely distributed. One branch of the tribe, which is mainly Sikh, is found in Hoshiarpur: while another section, which adheres to Hinduism, is settled in the neighbourhood of Delhi. It is probable that the ancestors of the Hoshiarpur colony were emigrants from the former city. They shew indications of an eastern origin by their not practising *karéwa, i.e.*, widow-marriage, and by wearing the *janéo* at weddings.

25. The *Sohal* is an important tribe numbering about 30,000 of which about one-third are Sikhs. The *Sohal* are found chiefly in Amritsar and the Doába, but are also scattered in other districts. The clan is divided into four *muhins, viz.*, *Déo*, *Gúrú*, *Máhech*, and *Mángat*.

26. The *Sansi* or *Sindhanwalia* are one of the most influential clans of the Punjáb, and though nominally of Rájpút descent, it is more than probable that they are in some way related to the *Sánsiyas*, an aboriginal tribe of criminal vagrants. The Máháràja Ranjit Singh was a *Sánsi* and many of his attributes were not inconsistent with a *Sansiya* origin. The clan is small and is found chiefly in Amritsar.

* *Randháwa* is derived from *ran* 'war,' and *daurna* 'to run,' and means 'eager for war. The tribe has a good reputation for courage.

27. The *Sidhu* clan is the largest and most aristocratic of the Jat tribes of the Punjáb and traces its descent to a *Bhátti* Rájpút named Jai Sál, one of whose descendants, Khiwa, married a Jatni, by whom he had issue a son named Sidhu, who gave his name to the clan. The *Sidhus* are divided into numerous subdivisions called *muhins*, of which the *Barar* is the most important, and are found chiefly in the Málwa, though some have spread into the Mánjha and Doába districts. They number over 100,000 Sikhs, and as soldiers are second to none.

A famous scion of the *Sidhus*, called Phul, was the founder of the *Phulkián misl* or confederacy, composed of the chiefs of Patiála, Nábha Jhind, and Faridkót. The headquarters of the tribe are at Máharáj in the Ferozepur district, and the heir of every Phulkián State has to visit the village at least once in his life-time and perform the ceremony called *tilkára*, which consists of digging some earth from the village pond.

28. The *Sindhus* or *Sandhus* are found chiefly in the Lahore and Amritsar districts, but are scattered all along the Upper Sutlej, and under the hills from Umballa in the east, to Sialkót and Gújránwála in the west. They claim descent from the *Raghúbansi* branch of the Solar Rájpúts, through Rám Chandar, King of Ajudhya. They say that their ancestors were taken by, or accompanied Mahmúd to Ghazni, and returned during the 13th century from Afghánistán into India. It is possible, however, that the Ghazni of their traditions was really in the Dekhan, while some authorities suggest that it was Ghadni in Bikaneer. Sir Lepel Griffin is of opinion that the real origin of the tribe is from north-western Rájpútána. The *Sindhus* like the *Sahis* worship the *Jhand* tree, and have some curious marriage customs. The tribal divinity is Kála Pir, or Kála Mehr, who is supposed to have special influence over cows and is accordingly propitiated by offerings of milk. The *Sindhus* number about 100,000 Sikhs, and as regards fighting qualities, are described as "the pick of the Mánjha." They are divided into 84 *muhins*.

29. The *Tarar* and *Varaich* or *Chung* are large Jat tribes, but are now chiefly Muhammadans. Both claim a Rájpút origin.

30. The *Virk* claim descent from a Rájpút of that name who emigrated from Jummoo to the neighbourhood of Amritsar and married a Jatni of the *Gil* tribe by whom he had three sons,—Drigar, Virk, and Waran. The story of the younger Virk's courtship is exactly the same as that related of Akbar with reference to the *Dháliwál*. Before the young couple had been married a year, Virk died, and his wife, who was pregnant, was condemned as a *Sati* to burn with her husband's corpse. Just as the funeral pyre was lighted, the Jatni gave birth to a boy, who was rescued

by one of the onlookers. The lad, who was named Angiári by his protector was shortly afterwards poisoned by a Bráhman, but miraculously recovered When Angiári grew up, he entered the service of the Jummoo Rájas and became the founder of a Jat clan which established itself in Gújránwála and Lahore. The tribe numbers about 20,000 Sikhs and is of high standing.

BRAHMANS.

Shown in Map as 31.

The renunciation of caste which formed the fundamental principle of Gúrú Govind Singh's teaching, was naturally inimical to the ideas of the Bráhmans, whose intelligence taught them that they had little to gain from Sikhism. Bráhman Sikhs are consequently comparatively few, and the number enlisted is not large. Though individually often excellent soldiers, their enlistment is not generally desirable, as their influence over Sikhs of lower caste is apt to be detrimental to discipline, and to destroy the *raison d' être* of Sikhism. The Bráhmans of the Punjáb nearly all belong to the *Sarsút* or *Sáraswat* division, and more especially to one of its clans called *Mújhal.* These military Bráhmans have, as a rule, given up their sacerdotal character, cultivate lands, and either enlist in the police or become clerks. Their intelligence and education generally enables them to rise to the higher grades, and they nearly always make excellent pay havildars. They are found all over the Punjáb, but are most numerous in the Cis-Sutlej districts. Out of a total population of over a million, only 7,600 are Sikhs.

RAJPUTS.

Shown in map as 32.

In the Punjáb, Jat and Rájpút tribes are often so closely connected, that it is sometimes extremely difficult to determine to which of these races a tribe really belongs. Most authorities agree that Rájpúts and Jats belong to an Aryo-Scythian stock which entered India from the plains of Central Asia, and that they probably represent at least two separate waves of immigration. "But admitting this theory to be true, it is at least exceedingly probable, both from their almost identical physique and social character and the close communion which has always existed between them, that they belong to one and the same ethnic stock; while whether this be so or not, it is almost certain that they have been for many centuries, and still are, so intermingled and so blended into one people, that it is practically impossible to distinguish them as separate wholes."*

* Ethnography of the Punjab.—*Denzil Ibbetson.*

Under the Sikhs, the Rájpút was overshadowed by the Jat, who resenting his assumption of superiority, and his refusal to join him on equal terms in the ranks of the *Khálsa*, deliberately persecuted him wherever and whenever he had the power. Under the circumstances it is not to be wondered at that the number of Rájpút Sikhs is but small. The few who have adopted the faith of Gúrú Govind are met with in Gurdaspur and Sialkót, but are found chiefly in the Hoshiarpur district, the birthplace of Sikhism, where they have adopted agriculture and lost the extreme pride of race which is generally their most prominent characteristic. They are accorded a high social position, and make excellent soldiers though the number now serving is but small.

Out of a Rájpút population of a million and-a-half, only 20,000 are Sikhs. The following are their principal divisions :—

Awan.	Chauhán.	Kharral.	Manj.	Tarár.
Bhatti.	Chhadhar.	Khokar.	Rahtor.	

KHATRIS.

Shown in map as 33.

The Khatris claim a Rájpút or Kshatriya descent, but nowadays their principal occupation is commerce, though many cultivate their own lands. " Besides monopolising the trade of the Punjáb and Afghánistán and doing a good deal beyond those limits, they are, in the Punjáb, the chief civil administrators, and clerical work is almost entirely in their hands. So far as the Sikhs have a priesthood, they are, moreover, their priests and *Gúrús*. Both Nának and Govind were, and the *Sódhis* and *Bédis* are Khatris. They are not usually military in their character, but are quite capable of using their swords when necessary." Diwán Sáwan Mal, Governor of Mooltán, and his notorious successor, Múlráj, were Khatris; and Hari Singh, who was considered one of the best generals in the *Khálsa* army, also belonged to this class. In the Punjáb " no village can get on without its Khatri who keeps the accounts, does the banking business, and buys and sells the grain. In Afghánistán among a rough and alien people, the Khatris are, as a rule, confined to the position of humble dealers, shopkeepers, and moneylenders; but in that capacity the Patháns seem to look on them as a kind of valuable animal, and a Pathán will steal another man's Khatri not only for the sake of ransom, as is sometimes done on the Peshávar and Hazára frontier, but also as he might steal a milch-cow or as Jews might, I dare say, be carried off in the Middle Ages with a view to render them profitable. The Khatris are staunch Hindus, and it is somewhat singular that, while giving a religion and priests to the Sikhs, they themselves are comparatively seldom of that persuasion. The Khatris are a very fine, fair, and handsome race, and are generally very well educated."*

There are colonies of Khatri Sikhs in the Miranzai, Swat, and Tirah valleys, where they live as *hamsáyas* or retainers of the Patháns amongst whom they have settled. They are supposed to be descendants of refugees who, about 1756, sought an asylum in the hills from the tyranny of Ahmad Shah† and his son Timur. They have not dropped any of their Sikh customs. A few have been enlisted from time to time in the army and border police, where their knowledge of Pushtu and local topography makes them valuable soldiers when employed on frontier service.

The Khatri Sikh who enlists nearly always prefers service in the cavalry, where his individual smartness and intelligence gives him a great advantage over the honest but rather thickheaded Jat. The Khatris most partial to military service are those belonging to the Gújránwála, Rawal Pindi and Jhelum districts, where they are landowners rather than traders.

The Khatris are divided into four principal clans,‡ as follows :—

Bunjahi.	Bahri.
Sarin.	Kohkran.

Besides the above, there are numerous social divisions, such as the *Dhaighar*, *Charzáti* and *Chhezáti*, which are again split up into various families and septs.

The *Bunjahi* Khatris owe their influence and importance to the fact that they include the *Bédi* and *Sódhi* clans, to which belonged the founders of the Sikh faith. Gúrú Nának was a *Bédi*, while the remaining *Gúrús*, from Rám Dás onwards, were *Sódhis*.

Khatris are most numerous in the Ludhiána, Hoshiarpur, Amritsar, Lahore, Gújránwála, Rawalpindi, and Jhelum districts. The total Khatri population, is 447,000, of which 52,000 are Sikhs.

* Ethnology of India.—*Campbell.*

† This was Ahmad Shah Abdáli, a Saddozai Afghán, who, in 1747, on the death of his master Nadir Shah, was crowned King of Kábul, with the title of Durri Durráni or 'Pearl of Pearls.' He repeatedly invaded India, and by marrying his son Timur to the daughter of the Delhi Emperor, gained as her dowry the whole of the Punjáb and Lahore.—The Races of Afghánistán.—*Bellew.*

‡ According to Falcon the names of the chief Khatri clans are Marhotra or Mahra, Khanne, Kapur, and Seth.

Khatris, being the hereditary priests of the Sikhs, are strict in the observance of the ordinances of their religion, and make excellent regimental *Granthis*. They have a high social position by caste, and make good soldiers if recruited from the agricultural class.

Aroras.

Shown in map as 34.

The Arόras claim to be of Khatri origin and say that they became outcasts from the Kshatriya, or Rájput stock, during the persecution of that people by Parashu or the 'axe-armed Ráma,' the last incarnation of Vishnu, and the special protector of Bráhmans. To escape his wrath, the Arόras denied their caste, and described themselves as '*aur*' or 'another,' hence their name. It is probable, however, that the name Arόra is really derived from Arόr, now Rori, the ancient capital of Scinde. The tribe is divided into two principal branches—the *Uttaráddhi* descended from families who fled northwards, and the *Dekhana* from those who escaped to the south. The *Uttaráddhi* branch is subdivided into two minor septs called *Báhri* and *Bunjáhi*, which correspond with similarly named Khatri clans, and thus confirm the theory of the Arόra connection with that tribe. The *Dekhana* are split up into two subdivisions—the *Dahra* and *Dakhanadháin*. The *Báhri* and *Dakhanadháin* claim social superiority over all other septs of the tribe.

The Arόra is the trader *par excellence* of the south-western portion of the Punjáb. More than half the Arόras dwell in Mooltán and the Deraját. The remainder are scattered throughout the Doába and Mánjha districts. Like the Khatri, and unlike the Banya, the Arόra is no mere trader; but his social position is far inferior to theirs, chiefly, no doubt, because his special *habitat* is among the frontier Muhammadans by whom all Hindus are held in the greatest contempt. He is commonly known as a *Kirár*, a word which is almost synonymous with 'coward.' The word *Kirár*, indeed, appears to be applied to all Punjábi traders whether Khatris or Arόras, to distinguish them from the Banyas and Mahájans of Hindustán. The occupational distinction between a Khatri and an Arόra is that while the former is usually a contractor, official, or accountant, the latter, as a rule, is only a petty trader. The Arόra is active, enterprising, industrious, and thrifty, and will turn his hand to any work. He is found throughout Afghánistán and even in Túrkistán, and is the Hindu trader of those countries. The proverbs* of the Punjáb peasantry are full of allusions to the cowar-

* "Trust not a crow, a dog, or a Kirár, even when asleep."
"To meet a Ráthi armed with a hoe makes a company of nine Kirárs feel alone."

dice and treachery of this tribe. Aróras are of inferior physique and their character is thus summed up: "a cowardly, secretive, acquisitive race, very necessary and useful in their way, but possessed of few manly qualities and both despised and envied by the great Musalmán tribes of Bannu."* About 9 per cent. of the Aróras are Sikhs, the remainder being Hindus.† Some of the latter however, especially on the Sutlej and Lower Indus, are really *Munna, i.e.*, shaven Sikhs, or followers of Bába Nának, while others either worship the Krishna incarnation of Vishnu, or the Indus river itself, under the names of Khwája Khizr and Zinda Pir. The Aróra, whether Sikh or Hindu, is generally unsuited for military service, and men of this class should never be enlisted except under special circumstances.‡

LABANAS.

Shown in map as 35.

Labánas enjoy among Sikhs much the same status as Mahtons whom they closely resemble. The Labánas of the Punjáb correspond to the Banjáras of Hindustán and the Dekhan, and were formerly largely employed by Khatris and Aróras as carriers of grain and merchandise. The spread of railway communication has dealt a death blow to their carrying trade, and many are now merchants and agriculturists. The Banjáras were formerly great suppliers of carriage, and Indian armies, from the time of the Mughals to that of Lake and Wellesley, were largely dependent upon them for supplies and transport. Physically and intellectually there is but little to choose between Labánas and Jats. They possess great courage and endurance, and their hereditary connection with the carrying trade renders them very knowledgeable in matters relating to transport. The esteem with which the Labána is regarded by the Jat is greater than that which his social position would warrant. Labánas are enlisted chiefly in the Pioneer regiments; those who are Sikhs are imbued with a spirit of martial ardour and possess most of the qualifications required in an infantry soldier. They are found chiefly in the Lahore, Gújránwála, Sialkot, Gurdaspur, and Gujrat districts, and have a large colony in Baháwalpur, where they are mostly *Munnas, i.e.*, followers of Bába Nának. About 33 per cent. of the total numbers of the tribe are returned as Sikhs.§ They have somewhat Gipsy habits and when conversing together speak a language foreign to Panjábi.

---

* Punjab Ethnography.—*Denzil Ibbetson.*

† The Census Report of 1891 gave the Aróra population as 667,000, of which 60,000 were recorded as Sikhs.

‡ It is only fair to add, however, that it is stated by one authority that "the Aróras who reside in the Punjáb proper make very fair soldiers, and are not the despicable people above described. They could if required be enlisted with Khatri Sikhs, with whom, however, they would compare as a rule unfavourably."

§ According to the Census Report of 1891 there are 18,000 Labána Sikhs out of a total population of 56,000. Many of them are *Sajdháris* or *Nánakpanthis.*

MAHTAMS, MAHTONS, OR BAHRUPIAS.

Shown in map as 36.

This is a low caste tribe of vagrants and hunters, found chiefly on the banks of the Punjáb rivers, more especially the Sutlej, where they pick up a living by snaring animals. In the Sutlej Doáb, however, they have devoted themselves to agriculture, and are skilful and laborious cultivators. Here they are always called Mahtons, profess to be fallen Rájpúts, and disown all connection with the outcast Mahtams of the western districts. In appearance they are short and dark, though frequently of sturdy build; in character they are said to be quarrelsome and litigious. About one-third* of the tribe profess to be Sikhs, and as such have occasionally been enlisted. They make fair soldiers, but are always looked down upon by the Jats. Their principal clans or *gots* are as follows:—

Dupaich.	Púri.	Matiai.	Gughial.
Khatti.	Sahsarvai.	Khattán.	Thindal.
Barár.	Karsúdh.	Gaihind.	Papla.
Sakrél.	Bábat.	Sháfan.	Jhalwál.

The Western Mahtams are sometimes known as *Rassibat.*

SAINIS.

Shown in map as 37.

The Sainis in the Punjáb correspond to the Mális or gardeners of the North-West Provinces. They are found chiefly along the foot of the hills, between the valleys of the Jumna and Rávi, and in portions of Umballa, Jullundur, and Hoshiarpur. About 10 per cent.† of their number are Sikhs, chiefly in the last named districts. Sainis are most industrious cultivators, producing three and sometimes four crops within the year from the same garden-plot. They have proved good soldiers, orderly and well behaved, but they do not possess the military qualities of the Jats, who are very much their social superiors. The following are the names of their principal clans:—

Bóli.	Hamarti.	Mangar.
Páwán.	Badwál.	Badyal.
Gaddi.	Alagni.	Baryal, or Baigal.
Salahri.	Mangar.	

A Saini village can generally be distinguished by the quantity of pepper drying on the roofs of the houses.

* There are about 17,000 Mahton Sikhs. † There are nearly 18,000 Saini Sikhs.

KAMBOHS.

Shown in map as 38.

The Kambohs are one of the finest cultivating classes in the Punjáb. They are found all over the province, but more especially in Kapurthala. The name of the tribe is said to be a corruption of *Kai-amboh*, 'the assembly of the *Kai*,' a royal race of Persia from which they profess to be descended. The Muhammadan Kambohs were powerful and influential in the early days of the Mughal Empire. A Kamboh general, named Sháhbáz Khan, was one of Akbar's most trusted officers, and distinguished himself greatly in Bengal. The Hindu Kambohs profess to be related to Rájpúts and to have come from Persia through Southern Afghánistán. They state that many of their ancestors were forcibly converted to Islám by Mahmúd of Ghazni. The Kambohs are not, as a rule, in good odour with the communities to which they belong. One critic describes them as "turbulent, crafty, stiff-necked, and as such more akin to Afgháns than any of the Hindu races of the plains amongst which they have now been settled for many generations." About 23 per cent. of the Kambohs are Sikhs, and the latter, who are rapidly increasing, now number about 45,000.

The following are the names of their principal clans:—

Thind.	Dahút.	Jammún.
Junsan.	Mahrok.	Jhande.
Jaura.	Sande.	Unmál.

All the above clans are suitable for enlistment as they are generally industrious and of powerful physique.

KALWARS, KALALS, OR AHLUWALIAS.

Shown in map as 39.

The Kalál or Kalwár, as he is generally called in the Western Punjáb, is a hereditary distiller and seller of spirituous liquors. But since the manufacture and traffic in spirits has been subjected to Government regulation, a large proportion of the clan, and more especially the Sikh and Muhammadan sections, have abandoned their proper calling, and taken to other pursuits. Kaláls are renowned for their energy and enterprise. Their obstinacy is referred to in a well-known proverb—"Death may budge, but a Kalál won't." The original social position of the clan was an extremely humble one, but in the Punjáb it has been raised by special circumstances. The reigning family of Kapúrthala is descended from one Sada Singh,

Kalál, who founded the village of Ahlu near Lahore. The family gradually rose in the social scale, and Badar Singh, the great grandson of Sada Singh, married the daughter of a petty *Sardar* of the district. From this union sprang Jassa Singh, who was the most powerful and influential chief that the Sikhs possessed until the rise of Ranjit Singh. He adopted the title of Ahlúwália from the name of his ancestral village, and it is still retained not only by the Kapúrthala family, but very generally by all Sikh Kaláls. There are about 48,000 Kaláls in the Punjáb, of whom over 9,000 are Sikhs. Men of this clan are physically and intellectually but little inferior to Jats, and they generally make excellent soldiers. The Kaláls of the Mánjha, Kapúrthala, and Patiála are probably the best. They are sometimes called *Neb*.

Tarkhans or Ramgarhias.

Shown in map as 40.

The Lohár or blacksmith, and the Tarkhán or carpenter, are closely allied, and rank highest among the village menials. Though separate castes, they are probably of the same origin, and in most parts of the Punjáb intermarry. The Tarkhán, also called Kháti, corresponds to the Barhai of the North-West Provinces. He manufactures and repairs the agricultural implements and household furniture required in his village, making them all, except carts, Persian-wheels, and sugar presses, with little remuneration beyond his customary dues, which are generally paid in kind. Though practically of the same caste, the social position of the Tarkhán is distinctly superior to that of the Lohár. Sikh Tarkháns always call themselves Rámgarhias in remembrance of a famous ancestor called Jassa Singh, who was the leader of the Rámgarhia *misl* or confederacy, and the builder of the Rámgarh or citadel of Amritsar. Many Rámgarhias are cultivators and hold respectable positions. The tribe is distributed throughout the Punjáb and includes in its total population some 134,000 Sikhs. Tarkháns seldom enlist as they can earn higher wages by working at their trade. The following are the principal septs of the clan :—

Dháman.	Matháru.	Netál.
Khatti.	Gáde.	Janjúa.
Siáwán.	Tháru.	Khokhar.

Many Tarkháns now become *Granthis*. As a class they are intelligent and well educated.

NAIS.

Shown in map as 41.

The Nai is the village barber, and corresponds to the Musalmán Hajjám of the cities. His occupation is a menial one, his duties being to shave and shampoo the villagers, prepare tobacco* for the village rest-house, and attend upon the village guests. But he is really much more than a barber. He is the hereditary bearer of formal messages from one village to another, such as news of auspicious events, formal congratulations, and letters fixing the dates of weddings, etc. News of a death is never carried by him, but always by a Chúhra. He, in company with a Bráhman, acts as the *lagi* or 'go-between' in the negotiations which precede a betrothal. At marriage ceremonies too, he plays an important part, next indeed to that of the Bráhman himself, and on all these occasions receives suitable gratuities. He is also the leech and village surgeon, and among Muhammadans, performs the ceremony of circumcision. Nothwithstanding all this, the Nai is essentially a *kamin* or village servant, of much the same social standing as the Dhóbi, far above the Chamár, but somewhat below the Lohár, for his occupation as a barber proper is considered degrading. The outcast tribes have their own Nais, for a Nai who has shaved a Chúhra would not be permitted to touch a Jat. The Nais are popularly regarded as extremely astute. "The jackal," says the Punjáb villager, "is the sharpest amongst beasts, the crow among birds, and the Nai among men." The tribe is found throughout the Punjáb and has a population of about 340,000, of which over 20,000 are Sikhs. A Sikh barber would appear to be rather an anomaly, but it must be remembered that in addition to his more usual functions he shampoos, cuts the nails, and cleans the ears of his clients. His village name, in fact, is *Naherna*, the 'nail-cutter.' The Nai Sikh was frequently enlisted as a soldier in former days, but, in common with other humble classes of Sikhs, has been gradually displaced by the Jat. The following are the principal *gots* of the tribe:—

Góla.	Bahgu.
Bhanbhéru.	Bhátti.
Bási.	Khokhar.

The village barber-surgeon is sometimes called *Jarrah.*

CHHIMBAS, NAMABANSIS, OR BARETAS.

Shown in map as 42.

The Chhimba or calico-printer is closely associated with the Dhóbi or washerman; both belonging to the same tribe, though the occupation of the

* Unless he is a true Govindi Sikh, in which case the touching of tobacco would be forbidden.

former is considered slightly less degrading than the latter. The Dhóbi is a true village menial in the sense that he receives a fixed share of the produce in return for washing the clothes of the villagers wherever he performs that office. He only occupies this position, however, among the higher castes of landowners; for among the Jats, and classes of similar standing, the washing is generally done by the women of the family. His social position is very low, for his occupation is considered impure, and he alone, of the tribes which are not outcast, will imitate the Kumhár in keeping and using a donkey. He stands below the Nai, but perhaps above the Kumhár. The Chhimba is properly a stamper of coloured patterns on the cotton fabrics of the country, but, as has before been remarked, he can hardly be distinguished from the Dhóbi. Besides being a printer, he dyes in madder, leaving other colours, more especially indigo,* which is an abomination to all Hindus, to his Musalmán *confrére* the Lilári or Rangréz. The patron saint of the Sikh and Hindu Chhimbas is a worthy named Bába Námdeo, who lived at Batála in Gurdaspur towards the end of the 15th century. The Chhimba or *Námabansi* Sikh, as he is occasionally called in his village, was at one time freely enlisted, and made a tolerably efficient soldier. Care should be taken not to confound him with the *Chima* who is a Jat of very good standing. The following are the principal septs of the tribe :—

Sippal.	Khokhar.
Bhátti.	Kamboh.

There are about 144,000 Chhimbas in the Punjáb, but only 23,000 are Sikhs. Chhimbas are also known by the names of Chipi, Chhibú, and Chápagar. Many Chhimbas have now taken to tailoring and Sikh *dárzis* are generally of this class.

JHIWARS, JHINWARS, KAHARS, OR SAKKAS.

Shown in map as 43.

The Jhinwar of the Eastern Punjáb corresponds to the Kahár of the North-West Provinces, and the Musalmán Máchhi of the trans-Sutlej districts. The Jhinwar, who is generally called Mahra among the Sikhs, is a carrier, waterman, fisherman, and basket-maker. He also carries palanquins, and all such burdens as are borne by a yoke on the shoulders. He is especially concerned with the cultivation of waternuts, the netting of waterfowl, and the sinking of wells. He is a true *kamin* or village menial, receiving customary dues in return for customary service. In this capacity he supplies all the baskets needed by the cultivator, and brings water to the men in the fields at harvest time, to the houses where the

* For further particulars regarding this curious superstition see page 63.

women are secluded, and attends to the guests at weddings and on similar occasions. His social standing is in one respect high; for all will drink at his hands, and all will eat the food he has cooked. He is nevertheless a servant, though perhaps the highest of that class. The Jhinwar seldom works in the fields except for pay at harvest time, when the rice is being planted out, or on other special occasions. Besides the occupations already described, the Jhinwar is the cook, and his wife the *accoucheuse* of the Punjáb proper. *Dáyis* and wet-nurses are nearly always of the Jhinwar caste. Moreover the common oven, which forms so important a feature in the village-life of the Punjáb, and at which the peasantry have their bread baked in the hot weather, is almost always in the hands of a Jhinwar, who is also the village woodcutter. Sikhs of this class have been known to make very good soldiers, and a few may be enlisted without harm, for the sake of their general utility. In Sikh regiments the Jhinwar is employed as a Lángri or regimental cook in preference to any other class. If he carries water in a skin he is called a Sakká, and if in earthen or brass vessels a Kahár. The primary occupation of the Kahár is carrying litters. From this, and from the fact that they are 'clean' Súdras, Kahárs are employed as servants by all respectable Sikhs and Hindus, and are largely enlisted by the Commissariat-Transport Department for service in Native Hospitals.

RAMDASIAS.

Shown in map as 44.

The Rámdásia is now generally a weaver, but is of the same tribe as the Chamár or leather-dresser. The open adoption of a definite faith by outcast classes such as the Chúhra and Chamár is, as a rule, the first step made in their upward struggle, and is very commonly accompanied by the abandonment of their old occupation for one which stands higher in the social scale. Thus the Chúhra scavenger on becoming a Musalmán will refuse to remove nightsoil, and on becoming a Sikh will take to tanning and leather work. The tanner and leather worker on becoming a Muhammadan will give up tanning, and on taking the Sikh *pahúl* will turn his hand to the loom, and so forth. The Hindu reformation which produced Sikhism, also produced many *Bhagats*, or religious leaders of low caste origin, who taught the people the principles of religion in their own vernaculars, instead of in the unintelligible Sanskrit of the Bráhmans. Among these *Bhagats* were Kabir (a Juláha), Nám Deo (a Chhimba), and Rávi Dás (a Chamár). Their writings are constantly quoted in the *Adi Granth*. One of the reforms contemplated and partially carried out by Sikhism was the abolition of caste, carrying with it a general permission to study the Hindu scriptures, a privilege which was extended even to such outcasts as Chúhras and Chamárs.

Taking advantage of this concession, some of the lowest classes became Sikhs. They gave up their degrading occupations and took to other means of livelihood. They also changed their name, and gave up social intercourse with the unconverted members of their tribe as far as they possibly could. Thus the Chamárs on their conversion to Sikhism took the name of Rávi Dás, the first *Bhagat* of their race, to show that they followed his example. *Rámdásia* is only a corruption of Rávdásia, the correct form of the word. Similarly Chhimba Sikhs call themselves *Námabansis* after their great leader, Nám Deo. In the present day if a Chamár takes the *pahúl* and becomes a Sikh, he at once joins the Rámdásias. The latter will only marry the daughters of ordinary Chamárs, conditionally on their taking the *pahúl.* A Rámdásia would not drink water from the hands of an ordinary Chamár, unless the latter became a Sikh. Some authorities are of opinion that Rámdásias take their name, not from the Bhagat Rávi Dás, but from Rám Dás, the 4th *Gúrú* of the Sikhs, who was the first to accept Chamárs as converts. Rámdásias are found chiefly in the Doába and Málwa districts, where they are mostly field labourers, and are enlisted in small numbers in the 23rd, 32nd and 34th Pioneers. They have proved good soldiers in spite of their lowly origin, but are seldom of robust physique. Many Rámdásias are *Nánakpanthis*, few are true *Pahúlias.*

MAZBHIS, RANGRETAS, OR CHUHRAS.

Shown in map as 45.

The Chúhra of the Punjáb corresponds to the Bhangi of Hindústán and is *par excellence* the sweeper and scavenger of the village community. He is found throughout the province, being most numerous, however, in Ferozepore, Lahore, Amritsar, and Faridkót, where much of the agricultural labour is performed by men of this caste. As one of the regular village menials, he receives a customary share of the produce of each harvest, and in return performs certain indispensable offices for his clients of higher caste. In the Eastern Punjáb he sweeps the houses and village, collects cowdung, kneads it into cakes and stacks it, works up the manure, helps with the cattle, and takes them from village to village. In the Sikh districts he adds to these functions actual hard work at the plough and in the fields. He claims the flesh of such animals as do not divide the hoof, the cloven-footed belonging to his humble *confrére* the Chamár.

The civilising effect of Sikhism in raising the social position of the lowest classes has already been noticed under the heading of Rámdásia, and finds an admirable illustration in the person of the Mazbhi or Chúhra convert to Sikhism. As a simple Chúhra, the Hindu sweeper occupies the lowest place in the social scale; he is avoided by all, and his merest touch is regarded as pollution. Converted to Sikhism, however, he to a large extent frees himself from the thraldom of his degraded position. He is still a village menial, but he is no longer the remover of night soil. He takes the *pahúl*, wears his hair long, abstains from tobacco, and strives by a rigorous and punctilious observance of all Sikh customs and ritual, to blot out the memory of his former degradation.

The highest classes of Mazbhis profess to be descended from three Chúhras who gallantly rescued the body of Tegh Bahádur from a Muhammadan mob, after the *Gúrú* had been cruelly executed at Delhi by the fanatical Emperor Aurangzéb. The three sweepers, on their return to Amritsar with the martyr's corpse, were at once baptized into the Sikh faith by Gúrú Govind Singh, who, in recognition of their valour and devotion, gave them the title of Mazbhi or 'faithful.' Many Mazbhis, however, are supposed to be descended from Muhammadans who were forcibly converted to Sikhism in the time of Ranjit Singh. Owing to the intense hatred of the Sikhs for Islám, most of these converts were classed with Chamárs and Chúhras; and as the first Chúhras admitted to the faith of the *Khálsa* had been given the title of Mazbhi, the same title was also applied to their converted Muhammadan associates. True Mazbhis are generally short, with black shiny skins, high cheek bone, flat noses, and a distinctly aboriginal type of face.

We hear little of the Mazbhi Sikhs during the troubled times following the decline of the Mughal Empire, but during the reign of Ranjit Singh they were extensively enlisted in the *Khálsa* army, being generally stationed on the Peshávar border where constant fighting gave them ample opportunities of showing their bravery and endurance.

After the British occupation of the Punjáb, the Mazbhis degenerated into a criminal tribe of thugs, robbers, and dacoits. About 1851 the Máháraja Guláb Singh of Kashmir established a corps of Mazbhis, which he employed in overawing his Muhammadan subjects. About the same time two Mazbhi coolie corps were raised, one for employment on the construction of the Grand Trunk Road, and another for similar work in Ceylon. On the outbreak of the Mutiny, the Mazbhis were still regarded as a criminal class and it was thought advisable to send them out of the Punjáb by forming them into pioneer regiments for service against the mutinous sepoys. Their extraordinary bravery, endurance, and patience under great and protracted privations, soon won for them a high reputation as soldiers—a reputation which has increased by their subsequent achievements in China, Abyssinia, Afghánistán, and numerous campaigns on the frontier.

The descendants of the Chúhra converts of Govind Singh sometimes describe themselves as *asl* Mazbhis to distinguish them from their Chúhra brethren whose conversion to Sikhism is more recent. In some districts, more especially in Umballa and Ludhiána, certain Mazbhis call themselves Rángrétas,* and profess to be socially superior to the rest of the tribe. These distinctions, however, are more theoretical than real, for the *asl* Mazbhi, once satisfied as to the genuineness of a Chúhra's conversion, accepts him as a brother, and will eat and drink with him without objection. Moreover, it is generally admitted by the Mazbhi *Granthis* themselves that a Chúhra family which has embraced Sikhism and scrupulously adhered to its tenets, is, after the second generation, unquestionably entitled to rank with the best of the original Mazbhis.† In some of the pioneer regiments Chúhra converts to Sikhism are called Málwais,‡ a somewhat misleading term, as it really means an inhabitant of the Málwa. It is probable that this practice arose from the fact that those first enlisted came from the cis-Sutlej districts, but the term is now applied indiscriminately to all who are Mazbhis by conversion, in contradistinction to those who are Mazbhis by descent. As a matter of fact Chúhras and Mazbhis, like any other Sikhs, may be either Manjhails or Málwais, according as they are recruited from the districts west or east of the Sutlej.

Until recently Mazbhis were not found in large numbers in any particular locality, being scattered in groups of two or three families through the Jat villages, where they worked as labourers for the owners of the soil. Government however, recognizing the advisability of separating them from communities where their position was menial and degrading, has now formed colonies of Mazbhi pensioners in the Gújránwála district, near the Chenáb where grants of land enable them to practise agriculture, and thus escape from a relapse to the humble position which they would hold among the Jats. This arrangement is not only of advantage as a means of rewarding deserving soldiers, but is also calculated to result in the formation of a really valuable recruiting-ground.

DEKHANI SIKHS.

Reference has been made on page 19 to the Sikh colony at Naderh on the Godávery, where Govind Singh met his death in 1708. The total number of Sikhs in the Dekhan is 4,637, and they are found chiefly in Naderh itself and in Hyderabad, Aurangabad, Digloor, and Mundnoor. These Dekhani Sikhs and mostly the descendants of Sikh pilgrims from the Punjáb

* Rángréta is said to mean 'like a Rángar.' The Rángars are a class of Musalmán Rájpúts renowned for their bravery.

† This statement is, however, open to question, for many authorities declare that the *asl* Mazbhi holds aloof from the Chúhra, and that the latter's conversion to Sikhism makes little difference in his social condition for some generations.

‡ It has been suggested that Málwai is a corruption of '*Málai*,' 'admitted,' in allusion to the story of their origin.

who first came to Naderh as worshippers at the *Gúrdwára* erected over Govind Singh's *Samád*, and, obtaining employment in the Dekhan, eventually formed colonies. They are now entirely localised, though recruited to a very limited extent from the Punjáb, and they intermarry among themselves.

The Dekhani Sikhs are initiated by taking the *pahúl*, and share in the *parshád* or communion. They are accepted as true Sikhs by their brethren of the Punjáb, but are considered as of an inferior class. About 1,200 of these Dekhani Sikhs are in the service of the Nizam—some in the Police and some in the Infantry. A certain number enlisted in the Central India Horse during the Mutiny, and the few now serving in the Hyderabad Contingent are reported to be fairly good soldiers.

The Dekhani Sikh is distinguishable from his Punjábi *confrére* by his dress, which is still much the same as it was in the time of Govind Singh. They wear the *kachh* or short drawers, and their head dress is the small tightly tied *pag* such as the Sikhs of the Punjáb now wear under the turban. As true Govindi Sikhs they are careful observers of the five *kakkás*, and conform strictly to the ordinances of the tenth *Gúrú*.

CHAPTER III.

RELIGION, CUSTOMS, SECTS, AND RELIGIOUS FESTIVALS.

RELIGION.

About the time of the Protestant Reformation in Europe, and before either the Mughals or Portuguese had appeared in India, a number of Hindu reformers, whose ideas had largely been influenced by Islám, strove to reform their religion by disowning caste, and by insisting on the unity of the godhead in lieu of the idolatrous polytheism encouraged and taught by the Bráhmans. In the 12th century, Rámaníya taught that Brahma was the omnipotent and omniscient Ruler of the Universe. Three hundred years later Vallabha, a disciple of the same school, taught that the human soul was like a spark from the Supreme Spirit, and though separate, was identical with it in essence. From these sects sprang various theistic movements of which the most important are those founded by Rámanand, Kabir, and the latter's famous disciple—Bába-Nának.

Hindu reformers of the 12th and 15th centuries.

The doctrines of the *Kabir-panthis* were undoubtedly initiated under the influence of Islám, and Kabir himself, who lived at the beginning of the 15th century, is believed to have been a Muhammadan. Unable to endure the intolerance of his own religion, he became a disciple of Rámanand, and, like the latter, was a true worshipper of Vishnu. He conformed to no rites, denounced idol worship, and taught Vaishnávism as a strict monotheism. The gist of his doctrines was that every man was bound to search for a true spiritual guide or *Gúrú*, and having found one, to submit his mind, conscience, and body, to his orders.

The Kabir-panthis.

Nának, the founder of Sikhism, was an ardent admirer of Kabir, whose utterances are constantly quoted in the *Granth*. Nának's main idea appears to have been the deliverance of Hinduism, and especially Vaishnávism, from its incubus of caste, superstition, and idolatry. He welcomed persons of all ranks as his followers, and taught that the Supreme Being was no respecter of persons. His beliefs, in fact, were partly Islámised. He lived among Muhammadans and became so imbued with the spirit of their faith, that his creed

The Sikhism of Nának.

became nothing more or less than an attempt to reconcile Hinduism to Islám on the common ground of a belief in a single God. It is curious that a religious movement which originated in a desire to draw Sikhs and Muhammadans together, should have ended in exciting the bitterest animosity between them.

Nának taught that the great object of human exertion was to avoid transmigration which is the principal object of apprehension to Hindu and Sikh alike. The Hindu doctrine is that all earthly actions, whether good or evil, carry with them their own reward or punishment. Those who have been altogether virtuous are received into the heaven of the deity which they have selected as the object of their particular devotion, and there they remain until their merit has worked itself out. Then the saint returns to earth and is reborn as a man under the most favourable conditions, his future being again determined by his conduct. If his life has been vicious or worldly he is thrown into purgatory, from which, after long periods of punishment, he is reborn in animal forms, the most degraded of which are reserved for the greatest moral turpitude. After countless transmigrations he again becomes a man and is able by virtuous conduct gradually to work off his former transgressions. "As the keys of heaven and hell were entrusted to Saint Peter and their presumed possession has given to the Church of Rome its immense vitality and influence, so the power of remission called *mukht*, claimed by the *Gúrú* in the matter of transmigration, has given to Sikhism the principal part of its attractiveness." This exemption from the common lot and the final resolution of the spirit of man into the Divine Essence is acquired by calling upon Hari, the name of the Supreme Being, by those who have been properly received into the faith and instructed by a properly appointed *Gúrú*.

Nának's doctrine regarding transmigration.

The most important doctrine of the *Adi Granth* is that of reverence and obedience to the *Gúrú*. The practices of ablution, of giving alms, of abstinence from animal food, are enjoined; while, as ethical teaching, evil speaking, unchastity, anger, covetousness, selfishness, and want of faith are specially denounced. Nának also taught that the position of a householder as head of a family and engaged in the business of the world was a most honourable one, and strongly discouraged the idea that any special virtue was to be gained by leading an ascetic life. He asserted that true religion consisted, not in outward ceremonial and the acceptance of the monastic habit, but in the feelings of the heart; and that it was possible to meditate with advantage on spiritual things while engaged in the ordinary business of life.

Moral precepts of the Adi Granth.

Although the *Adi Granth* is hostile to Bráhmans and altogether ignores or denies their pretensions, Nának did not directly enjoin the abolition of caste or remove the distinctions which it imposed. The only form of baptism which he adopted was the ordinary Hindu practice called *charan ghá-wal,** of drinking the water in which the feet of the *Gúrú* had been bathed, and even this soon fell into disuse.

The doctrines of Nának were scrupulously adhered to by his eight successors, and no change of any religious or social importance was introduced until the time of Gúrú Govind Singh. Rám Dás, who was Pontiff from 1574 to 1581, founded the *Darbar Sahib,* or Golden Temple at Amritsar. To Arjún, the fifth *Gúrú*, the Sikhs owe their Bible, the *Granth* or *Granth Sahib.* It was compiled about 1581, and besides the portions written by Nának and Arjún, includes extracts from the works of Kabir and Rámanand. This version of the *Granth* was subsequently called the *Adi Granth*† or First Book, to distinguish it from the *Daswén Badshah ki Granth*‡ written by Govind Singh, the tenth and last of the *Gúrús.*

From the days of Gúrú Arjún onwards, the Sikhs gradually drifted into greater opposition to the Imperial power, and in the time of Govind Singh (1675—1708), when the persecuting rigour of Aurangzéb was at its height, the Sikh community became transformed from a purely religious into a political association, and what was previously a quietist sect of Hindus into practically a separate religion.

The Sikhism of Govind Singh.

Govind Singh, though more inclined to polytheistic ideas than to the refined pantheism of Nának, did not desire or find it expedient to attack the doctrine of his great predecessor. What he wished was to consolidate the Sikh power, and to bring the Sikhs more completely out of the ranks of Hinduism so as to launch them with greater effect against Islám. His first step was to abolish the custom of caste upon which Bráhmanism is founded. This naturally brought upon him the wrath of the priests of that creed, and the dislike and suspicion of all the higher orders whose immemorial privileges were abridged or destroyed by the admission into the Sikh body of those whom they affected to despise.

---

* *Charan ghâwal* is a corruption of *Charan ka pahúl* or 'foot baptism' as opposed to the *khande ka pahúl* 'or baptism of the sword' which obtains among the Govindi Sikhs.

† The *Adi Granth* is written wholly in verse, but the forms of versification are numerous. The language used is rather the Hindi of Upper India than the particular dialect of the Punjáb; but some portions are composed in Sanskrit. The written character is nevertheless throughout the Punjábi, which, from its use by the Sikh *Gúrús*, is generally called Gúrmukhi.

‡ Like the *Adi Granth*, the *Daswén Badshah ki Granth* of Govind Singh is metrical throughout. It is written in the Hindi dialect of the Gangetic districts but in the Punjábi character except the concluding portion, the language of which is Persian while the alphabet used is Gurmukhi.

Besides the *Adi Granth* Govind Singh composed a work called the *Rahitnáma* or 'Book of Conduct.'

The other precepts of the *Gúrú* were made with the object of separating his followers from the general body of Hindus. They were principally rules of conduct regarding dress, food, and worship. Briefly speaking, Govind Singh added five points to the religion of Nának. Firstly, the

The Pahúl or Sikh oath of initiation.

ceremony of baptism was changed from the *charan ghâwal* to the *pahúl* or *amrit;* the Sikh no longer drank the water in which the feet of his *Gúrú* had been placed, but was solemnly initiated in the presence of five believers by drinking a mixture of sugar and water which had been stirred with a *khanda* or steel dagger. He then became a *Pahúlia* or *Khandadhári*, as opposed to a *Múnna*, and his name was altered by the addition of the distinctive title of *Singh.* Secondly, the Singh or warlike Sikh had to carry about his person

The outward signs of Sikhism.

five marks beginning with the letter *k*, which are known as the five *kakkás, viz.*, (1) the *khes* or uncut hair; (2) the *kachh* or short drawers; (3) the *kara* or iron bangle; (4) the *khanda* or steel dagger; and (5) the *kanga* or comb. Thirdly, the followers of Govind must abstain from smoking tobacco. Fourthly, they must not eat any meat except the flesh of animals which have been decapitated by a blow on the back of the neck called *jhatka.* And fifthly, they must not observe the distinctions of caste or pay special reverence to Bráhmans.

The kará parshád or sacramental food and communion of the Sikhs.

Govind also enjoined upon his followers the necessity for eating the *kará parshád*, or communion from a common dish, as an indication that they had abandoned the prejudices of caste.* He forbade the worship of shrines and temples, and the observance of Muhammadan and Hindu rites such as circumcision and the wearing of the Bráhmanical *janéo.*† The use of caps and saffron coloured garments was forbidden; the former because they were then only worn by Musalmáns, and the latter because saffron was the favourite colour of Hindu ascetics, a class from which he was anxious to separate his followers. Among minor injunctions may be noticed the prohibition against extinguishing fire with the breath, or with water part of which had been drunk; the necessity for wearing steel and a turban,

Minor injunctions of Govind Singh.

for bathing in cold water, for combing the hair twice a day, and for reading portions of the *Granth* morning, evening, and before meals. No one but a Sikh

* Among Sikh soldiers the *kará parshád* is generally celebrated once a month. Cakes of butter, flour, and sugar are made and consecrated with certain ceremonies, while the communicants sit round in prayer. The sacramental food is then distributed equally to all present.

† The *Janéo* or sacred thread is the emblem worn by the three highest castes of Hindus, *viz.*, Bráhmans, Rájpúts, and Vaisiyas, to symbolize their second or spiritual birth. It consists of three strings of spun cotton, varying in length according to caste. It is usually worn over the left shoulder and under the right arm, and its triple form is supposed to typify Bráhma, Vishnu, and Siva, the three persons of the Hindu Trinity, and Earth, Air, and Heaven, the three worlds pervaded by their essence.

was to be saluted, infanticide was strictly forbidden, and daughters were never to be sold in marriage.

Many of these observances have now fallen into disuse. They were devised by the *Gúrú* to separate his followers from their Hindu brethren and to stimulate their fanaticism against Muhammadans. Nowadays, with the exception of the *Akális*, who still scrupulously adhere to all the ordinances of Govind Singh, the ordinary Sikh peasant is content to take the *pahúl*, wear long hair, and abstain from tobacco. He still, however, partakes of the *kará parshád*, and eats no meat unless it has been killed by *jhatka*. The *kachh* are no longer worn except by *Kúkas*, *Akális*, and old men, as they interfere with the free use of the limbs and are not as comfortable for wear in the fields as the *dhóti*, which is wrapped round the loins like a kilt. The prohibition against receiving money for a daughter is also frequently evaded, while the modern Sikhs, particularly those of the Málwa, do not scruple to pay obeisance to Hindu divinities, and to make offerings at even Musalmán shrines. One of the most recent authorities on the subject states that "broadly speaking Sikhism may be described as Muhammadanism *minus* circumcision and cow-killing, and *plus* faith in the *Gúrús*."

Modern Sikhism.

Of the Hindu of whatever caste, it may be said as of the poet "nascitur non fit," his birth status being unalterable. But with the Sikh the exact reverse is the case. "Born of a Sikh father he is not himself counted of the faith until he has received the baptism of the *pahúl*.* Thus the supply of candidates for baptism is apt to rise or fall with the popular estimate of the advantages to be derived from joining the communion. During the days of Ranjit Singh when spiritual fervour and national pride worked in common, the numbers who joined the national faith were proportionately great. But after the British conquest of the Punjáb, Sikhism lost much of its old popularity. The *Khálsa* had fallen to rise no more, and its members were uncertain of the temper of their new masters, and as a consequence the Sikhs lay low, and refrained from bringing their sons to baptism. It was well, they argued, to watch the course of events, for the *pahúl* could be taken at any time."

The decay of Sikhism after the conquest of the Punjáb.

The Mutiny brought about an immediate revival of Sikhism. The followers of Govind were as eager as the British to restore order in Hindústán and to avert the threatened revival of the Mughal. The Sikhs found themselves no longer regarded with suspicion by their new masters,

* Strictly speaking the Sikh father cannot eat with his own son until the latter has taken the *Khande ká pahúl*.

but treated in a spirit of confidence and good fellowship. The name of Sikh became what it was in the days of Ranjit Singh, a title of honour, opening to its possessor the door of military service. Thus the creed received a new impulse. Many sons of Sikhs whose baptism had been deferred received the *pahúl*, while new candidates from among the Jats and lower castes joined the faith in considerable numbers.

The Sikh revival of 1857.

Since those days of enthusiasm, a reaction has naturally set in. The younger generation find the restrictions imposed on them by their religion, particularly in the matter of tobacco, most irksome. There are now no plundering forays or marauding expeditions, no cities to loot, or reprisals to be exacted from Muhammadans. Modern Sikhism, in fact, is to a large extent preserved from extinction by the encouragement it receives from the Indian Army, which, by exacting a rigorous observance of the outward signs of the religion from all its Sikh soldiers, keeps the advantages of the faith prominently before the eyes of the recruit-giving classes. "The chief cause of the decay of Sikhism is undeniably the strongly attractive force of Hinduism, which is always stronger in days of peace when martial aspirations are comparatively at a discount. The ivy-like vitality of Hinduism enfolds and strangles everything which it has once grasped. It has thus disposed of both Buddhism and Sikhism, each in its time a most formidable rival. Hinduism has ever been hostile to Sikhism, for the latter attacked it in its most vital principle of caste without which the whole Bráhmanical system falls to the ground. The influence of Hinduism, indeed, is doubly felt ; both in preventing the children of Sikh fathers from taking the *pahúl*, and by indirectly withdrawing professed Sikhs from the faith. By the performance of a few expiatory rites, the payment of a certain sum of money to Bráhmans, and the disuse of the military surname, the Sikh reverts as a Jat peasant into the ordinary Hindu community. Even where there has been no abandonment of the Sikh name and creed, the tendency is always in less essential matters to revert to the practice of the ancient religion, and it is here, as in all other countries, that feminine influence is paramount."

Present position of Sikhism.

The influence of Hinduism on Sikhism.

"To women, altogether uneducated, the abstract faith of Sikhism is far less attractive than Hinduism with its innumerable gods and childish legends, which, though ridiculous, are easily understood, and give to religious exercises a colour and life that the dry recital of the *Granth* can never impart. Joining in the Hindu worship, the Sikh women have their share in the outdoor life of the sisters in the village, the morning visit to the temple, or to the stones stained with red ochre where the protecting deity of the community resides; the numerous festivals of the Hindu calendar with the noise and excitement and fine clothes; these are the only diversions of native women whose lives are ordinarily sad and monotonous. Moreover the influence of the Bráhman priest weighs more heavily on the woman than on the man. He promises her children and that the proper observance of Hindu ritual will secure to her her husband's love, and guarantee her good fortune hereafter. The men are not exempt from the influence of the same sentiments. The old traditions of Bráhmanism are too strong for a new reforming creed like Sikhism to resist. The result is that the old order returns; the Sikh, although he will not smoke or cut his beard, pays reverence to Bráhmans and visits the temples and shrines of the old faith and observes the superstitious practices of other Hindus." Thus, in spite of the prohibitions against image worship, the Sikhs make an idol of their sacred book and worship and make offerings to the *Granth* just as Hindus do to their idols. In the matter of caste the Sikh retains the larger part of his freedom, but like the orthodox Hindu holds aloof from the unclean classes, and even the Mazbhi Sikhs are excluded from the Sikh shrines and are left to the religious ministration of *Granthis* of their own caste.

Preference shown by Sikh women for Hindu customs and beliefs.

The principal Sikh prayers are the *Japji*,* the *Rahras* † and the *Sohila*.‡ The *Japji* is read or repeated in the morning, the *Rahras* in the evening, and the *Sohila* before retiring to rest. Sikhs, like Hindus, generally go through their devotions alone, either in the village *dharmsála* or on the banks of any tank or stream in convenient proximity to their homes. They generally pray towards the east; never towards the south. The Mecca of the Sikhs is the Golden Temple or *Darbar Sáhib* at Amritsar. The causeway leading to this shrine is approached from a quadrangle facing the *Akál Bungah* or 'Pavilion of Immortality,' through an arched gateway called the '*Darshan Darwáza*' or 'Gate of Prayer.' A copy of the *Granth* is kept in the temple, watched over by attendant priests by whom passages from its pages are read morning and evening to the assembled worshippers. These attend in large numbers, especially at the great festivals. On the opening of the Sacred Book by the *Granthi*, silence reigns supreme. A few lines are read, at the end of which every man bows his head to the

Sikh prayers.

* *Jap* or *Japji* means literally 'the remembrancer,' from *jap*, to 'remember.'

† *Rahras* is a corruption of *Rech Ras*. *Rech* means an 'admonisher' and *Ras* is the name given to a recitation in honour of Krishna, one of the incarnations of Vishnu.

‡ *Sohila* means 'a song of rejoicing.'

ground with a murmur of gratification and respect. The book is then closed and reverently covered with silks.*

The initiation of Sikhs by the administering of the *pahúl* is generally carried out either in the *Akál Bungah* (where the weapons used by Govind Singh are kept in charge of *Akális* who are also entrusted with the care of the *Granth* at night) or at the Sikh shrines at Anandpur and Kiratpur in the Hoshiarpur district. Most Jat recruits, however, go through the ceremony on joining their regiments.

Hindu tendencies of the modern Sikhs.

Allusion has already been made to the tendency of modern Sikhism to conform in many respects to Hindu traditions and usage. The Sikh of to-day, more especially the Málwa Sikh, has fallen away from his original faith, and in his reverence for the Bráhman and his observance of caste rules, he differs only in degree from his orthodox Hindu neighbour. Both share the same superstitions, and both consider it necessary to propitiate the malevolent deities and godlings which harass the life of the Punjáb peasant. In the course of a few generations Sikhism is likely to be superseded by some form of Vaishnávism which is always most popular in times of peace.

The Hinduism of the Punjáb Jat.

The religion of the Punjáb Jat is a primitive form of Hinduism, but he is generally profoundly ignorant of the details of Puránic Mythology. He speaks of the Almighty as Parméshwar or Naráyan, but he takes but small heed of the great Trinity of his faith, and has acquired, probably from his Musalmán neighbours, a distinct bias in favour of monotheism, and his belief in the divinities whom he worships is often of the weakest. The existence of such a feeling of scepticism, however, is perfectly compatible with the most scrupulous care to neglect none of the usual observances, and whatever may be his convictions, a man would feel that it would be pre-eminently unsafe to omit the customary offerings, and that he would be running counter to public opinion if he did so.

The village godlings.

The village godlings with whom the peasant chiefly concerns himself may be broadly divided into two classes, the pure and the impure. To the former such offerings are made as are pure food to a Hindu, *viz.*, cakes, *chapátis*, and sweets fried in *ghi*. They are very generally presented on a Sunday, and are invariably taken by Bráhmans. To the second class the offerings are impure, such as the leavings of a meal, fowls, pigs, and so forth ; they are never

* The *Granth* used in *Dharmsálas* is kept on a small wooden stand called a *Mánji*, bedecked with silk coverings, with which it is carefully wrapped when not in use."

made on Sunday, and are taken by sweepers and other impure castes. The pure divinities are generally benevolent, the impure mischievous and spiteful.

Súraj Naráyan or Súraj Devata, the Sun God.

First among the pure and benevolent gods comes Súraj Naráyan or Súraj Dévata, the sun godling. The adoration of the sun is a *Védic* survival of the greatest antiquity. Among the more orthodox Hindus he is generally regarded as a manifestation of all three persons of the Hindu Trinity. In the east, at morning, he represents Bráhma or Creation; over head at noon he typifies Vishnu or Preservation; in the west at evening Siva or Destruction. To the Jat peasant, however, the sun is a godling rather than a god. No shrines are built in his honour, but on Sunday the people abstain from salt, and instead of setting their milk for *ghi*, offer it to Bráhmans and burn lamps in honour of the god. After each harvest, and occasionally between whiles, Bráhmans are fed in his honour, and the first care of the devout villager as he steps out of doors in the morning is to salute the sun, who is, *par excellence*, the favourite divinity of the rustic.

Worship of rivers, canals, and Khwája Khizr, the god of water.

After the sun comes the worship of the rivers. The Indus, Sutlej Ganges and Jumna, and even tributary canals, all come in for their share of the people's offerings. The Ganges is supposed to flow from Vishnu's feet, and to fall on Siva's head. The river is considered so sacred, that there is no sin, however heinous, which cannot be atoned for by bathing in its sacred depths; hence the traffic in Ganges water, which is transported in small bottles to the most distant parts of the country.* Khwája Khizr is properly a Muhammadan saint specially entrusted with the care of travellers; but in the Eastern and Central Punjáb he is the Hindu god of water, and is worshipped after the harvest and at the *Diwáli* and *Hóli* festivals by burning lamps, feeding Bráhmans, and setting afloat a miniature raft, bearing a lighted lamp. Of all the minor divinities, the Bhúmia or god of the homestead is perhaps the most important in the eyes of the Jat cultivator. As often as not, he is the spirit of the founder of the village, and his shrine is easily recognised by its domed roof which is generally close to the *dharmsála* or just outside the village site. The Bhúmia is worshipped on Sundays, at marriages, and on the birth of a son, by the burning of a lamp and the feeding of Bráhmans. The first milk of a cow or buffalo is always offered to this god.

Bhúmia or Khéra, the god of the homestead.

The worship of the sainted dead, though contrary to the injunctions of Govind Singh, is universal among Jats, whether Sikhs, Sultánis, or

* The river Deg in Gujránwála has become a rival to the Ganges, but only locally, and to a limited extent.

Hindus. Small shrines to *pitrs* or ancestors will be found all over the fields, and there is generally a large one to the *Jathéra* or common ancestor of the clan. Villagers who have migrated will periodically make long pilgrimages to worship at the shrine of their ancestor, or if the distance is too great, will bring away a brick from the original shrine and use it as the foundation of a new one. The fifteenth of the month is sacred to the *Pitrs*, and on that day the cattle should do no work and a number of Bráhmans must be fed. Besides the veneration of ancestors, saints of widespread renown occupy a very important place in the worship of the peasantry. They are generally Muhammadan, but are worshipped with the utmost impartiality by Hindus, Musalmáns, and Sikhs.

Worship of the Jathéra or ancestral shrine.

The three saints held in especial reverence in the Punjáb are Sakhi Sarwar Sultán, Bába Farid, and Gúga Pir. Of these, the first is by far the most important, and an account of his life, and of the doctrines of his followers, will be found on page 64 under the heading of Sikh sects. The shrine of Bába Farid at Pák Pattan in the Montgomery district, is celebrated throughout Muhammadan Asia. An annual fair takes place there on the fifth day of the Muharram, which is attended by thousands of Musalmán, Sikh, and Hindu pilgrims. The saint flourished about the early part of the 14th century, and his chief claim to distinction is that he is said to have nourished himself for thirty years by pressing wooden cakes and fruits to his stomach. Gúga Pir, also called Zahir Pir, was really a Hindu named Gúga Bir, or 'Gúga the Hero.' His name, however, has been altered, partly to suit the convenience of Muhammadan devotees, and partly because he is said to have himself become a convert to Muhammadanism. The story of this personage is that he was a Rájpút of Bikaneer who slew his brothers in a quarrel about some land, and was cursed by his mother in consequence. Wandering forth into the solitude of the desert, he called upon the earth to open and swallow him up, when a heavenly voice replied that this could only happen if he became a Muhammadan. He accordingly embraced Islám, and was then received into the bosom of the earth. The efficacy of prayers to this saint in cases of snake-bite, is much believed in. His symbol or standard is a pole, with a tuft of peacock's feathers at its summit.

The Muhammadan Saints.

The trees, plants and fruits reverenced by Sikhs and Hindus are the *túlsi* or holy basil; the *pipal;* the *bar;* the *bilva* or *bél;* the *váta* or banyan; the *amra* or mango; the *ním;* the *jhand;* the lotus; the cocoanut; and the

Plants and tree worship.

khúsa or sacred grass. The *pipal* and the *bar* are considered so sacred that only in the direst extremities of famine will their leaves be cut for the cattle. The latter is commonly selected to mark the shrine of a deity, and is employed in the marriage ceremonies of many of the Jat tribes.

The worship of the cow, and of peacocks and monkeys.

Among minor religious observances the first and foremost is the worship of the cow. "Of all animals it is the most sacred. Every part of its body is inhabited by some deity. Every hair on its body is inviolable. All its excreta are hallowed. Any spot which a cow has condescended to honour with the sacred deposit of her excrement, is for ever consecrated ground, and the filthiest place plastered with it is at once cleansed and freed from pollution, while the ashes produced by burning this substance are of such a holy nature that they not only make clean all material things, but have only to be sprinkled over a sinner to convert him into a saint." If a Sikh or Hindu be so unfortunate as to kill a cow by mishap, he has to go to the Ganges there to be purified at considerable expense. On the road he bears aloft the cow's tail, tied to a stick, so that all may know that he is impure, and unfit to enter a village. Monkeys and peacocks are generally regarded as sacred, the former because they are the representatives of Hanúmán the Monkey god, and the latter because they are the *protégés* of Skanda, one of the minor Hindu divinities.

The small-pox divinities.

Small-pox and kindred pustular diseases are supposed to be caused by a band of seven sisters, of whom Sitála or Máta is the greatest and most virulent. Others of the group are Dévi, Másáni, Basanti, Máha Mai, Polamde, Lamkaria, and Agwáni. There is generally a shrine to Sitála in every village. She is never worshipped by men, but only by women and children, generally on Mondays. During an epidemic of small-pox, no offerings are made; and if the disease has once seized upon a village, all offerings are discontinued until it has disappeared, as otherwise the evil will spread. So long, however, as she stays her hand, nothing is too good for the goddess. An adult, who has recovered from small-pox, should let a pig loose to Sitála, or he will be again attacked. The usual offerings to the goddess are fowls, pigs, goats, and cocoanuts, which are eaten by sweepers and Hindu *Jógis*.*

The malevolent dead include a number of godlings from whom nothing is to be expected and much is to be feared. Foremost among them are the

Gayáls.

Gayáls or sonless dead. When a man dies without male issue, his spirit becomes spiteful,

* *Jógis* are Hindu devotees "who among other tenets maintain the practicability of acquiring even in life command over elementary matter by certain ascetic practices."—Ethnographical Handbook.—*Crooke.*

especially seeking the lives of the sons of others. In almost every village small platforms may be seen with rows of small hemispherical depressions into which milk and Ganges water are poured, and by which lamps are lit, and Bráhmans fed, in order to assuage the *Gayáls.*

Bhúts.

Bhúts and *Churels* are the spirits of men and women who have died violent deaths, either by accident, suicide, or capital punishment, without the subsequent performance of proper funeral ceremonies ; the only way to propitiate them is to build shrines in their honour. Sweepers if buried mouth upwards are sure to become *Bhúts.* The small whirlwinds that raise pillars of dust in the hot weather are supposed to be *Bhuts* going to bathe in the Ganges. *Bhúts* are most to be feared by women and children, and especially after eating sweets. They have also a trick of going down the Hindu's throat when he yawns ; for this reason he should put his hand to his mouth and repeat the name of Naráyan.

Préts are the spirits of those who were deformed and crippled, or of persons who have not been dead for a year.

Pisácha are demons created by men's vices. All these demons must be propitiated by offerings of food, and the incantation of *mántras** by Bráhmans.†

Núris are fairies who attack women only, generally on moonlight nights. They are always Musalmánis, and must therefore be propitiated by offerings at Muhammadan shrines.

Minor superstitions.

The petty superstitions of the Punjáb are innumerable, but a few of the most important may here be mentioned. To sneeze is auspicious as it shows that you are unlikely to die for some time afterwards. Odd numbers are lucky with the exception of three and thirteen. "*Terah tin*" in fact is the Punjábi equivalent for "sixes and sevens." The number five runs through most ceremonial and religious customs. The south is the quarter to be specially avoided, as the spirits of the dead live there. On Sundays and Fridays one should not travel towards the west; on Saturdays and Mondays towards the east ; on Tuesdays and Wednesdays towards the north ; and on Thursdays towards the south. Thursday is a bad day for most things, but it is a favourable day for a soldier to leave his home to rejoin his regiment as it indicates that he will soon return. Sikhs and Hindu Jats will not grow indigo ; the latter dislike it because blue is the Muhammadan colour, and both have an aversion to touching it, because they say that it is

* *Mantras* are Sanskrit texts from the *Védas.*

† The more superstitious classes of natives regard *Máhámari* or plague as a *Rakshaha* or demon, let loose by the goddess Dévi to prey upon humanity as a punishment for sin and lack of faith.

the Chúhra or sweeper among plants.* One man will refuse to eat oil or black sesamum seed if formally offered by another, for if he accepted it, he would have to wait on his friend in the next life.

SIKH SECTS.

It has already been explained that Sikhism is of two kinds,— the simple theism of Nának which was marked by no outward signs, and the warlike faith of Govind which was indicated by the long hair and certain customs such as abstinence from tobacco, and the assumption of the title of *Singh*. The *Nánakpanthis* of to-day are known roughly as Sikhs who are not Singhs; *i.e.*, they are followers of the early *Gúrús* who do not think it necessary to follow the ceremonial and social observances inculcated by Gúrú Govind. Their characteristics are therefore mainly negative; they do *not* forbid smoking; they do *not* insist on long hair or the other four *kakkás*; they are *not* baptised with the *pahúl*; and they do *not*, even in theory, reject the authority of Bráhmans. The chief external difference between the *Nánakpanthi* or *Sajdhári* Sikh and the followers of Gúrú Govind Singh is in the disposal of the hair; the former, like the Hindu, shaves all but the scalp-lock called *bódi* or *chóti*, and hence is often known as a *Múnna* (shaven) or *Bódiwála* Sikh to distinguish him from the *Gobindi* or true Sikh who always wears long hair. The *Nánakpanthi* in fact, is little more than a lax Hindu who has been influenced by the teaching of the Sikh *Gúrús* and pays reverence to their sacred book the *Granth*.†

The Nánakpanthi Sajdhári or Munna, *i.e.*, *Shaven* Sikhs.

Here mention may be made of the followers of Sákhi Sultán Sarwar‡ commonly called *Sultánis*. The two religions of the Hindu Jats, *viz.*, Sikhism and the worship of Sultán Sarwar, do not really differ very much in practice. *Sultánis* are constantly taking the *pahúl*, and the conversion makes no difference to them except that they have to give up smoking. A *Sultáni* will generally call himself a Sikh§ and does not seem to recognize much difference between himself and the follower of Govind except that the latter cannot enjoy his pipe. The worship of Sultán Sarwar is one of the numberless signs of Musalmán influence which we come across in the daily life of the Hindu

Sultánis.

* Gazetteer of Ferozepore.

† The difference between the *Sajdhári* and the *Govindi* Sikh is stated in the *Sanskar Bagh* to be as follows: "Both are of the *Khalsa*, but the *Singh* worships God with *tun*, *mun*, and *dhan*, *i.e.*, with body, heart, and wealth, whereas the *Sajdhári* worships God with *mun* and *dhan* only."

‡ Sákhi Sarwar means 'the bountiful lord or chief, in allusion to the saint's generosity.'

§ The word Sikh is here used in its original sense of 'disciple,' and means that the Sultáni Jat is a disciple of Sákhi Sarwar, just is a Nánakpanthi Sikh is a disciple of Bába Nának.

peasant of the Punjáb. The traditions regarding his birth are rather vague, but the saint's family is believed to have emigrated from Bagdad to the Punjáb early in the 12th century, where, though himself a Muhammadan, he is said to have enlisted the Hindu God Bhairón as his messenger. The cult of the *Sultánis* is unsectarian in its creed, plastic in its observances and is in fact a sort of compromise between Hinduism and Islám. The shrines of Sarwar are known as *pirkhánas* or *tháns*. These unpretending little edifices are to be seen outside most hamlets in the Central and Eastern Punjáb. They generally consist of a hollow plastered brick cube, covered with a small dome, with low minarets at the four corners. The guardians of the shrines, called *Bharais*, are generally Muhammadans and go round on Thursdays beating drums and collecting offerings. A favourite method of pleasing the saint is to vow, a '*rót*' in his honour; 'the *rót*' being made by placing dough on a hot piece of earth where a fire has been burning, and distributing it as soon as it is properly baked. A special *rót* ceremony is also performed once a year, on a Friday, in most *Sultáni* families. A huge loaf is cooked containing a maund of flour and half maund of *gúr*. The priest sings the praises of the saint while it is preparing, and when it is ready takes a quarter for himself, and gives the rest to the family of his client. The principal *Sultáni* shrine is at Nigáha in the Déra Ghazi Khan district, and thousands of Sikh, Hindu, and Muhammadan pilgrims flock to the fair which is held there annually, many of them in the hope of, or in gratitude for, the birth of a son, a boon which is supposed to be specially in the gift of the saint.

The only observance which distinguishes Sarwar's followers from ordinary Hindu is that they will not eat the flesh of animals killed by *jhatka*, *i.e.*, a blow on the back of the neck. The *Sultáni*, if he eats meat at all, must eat animals whose throats have been cut in the orthodox Musalmán manner.* There is a prejudice against the enlistment of *Sultáni* Jats in Sikh regiments, but so long as they are willing to take the *pahúl*, there is no reason why they should not make excellent soldiers.

Besides *Nánakpanthis* and *Sultánis*, certain denominations have sprung up among the Sikhs which require to be briefly described. The *Udási* sect is an ascetic order which was founded by Sri Chand, the eldest son of Gúrú Nának. It is recruited from all classes and has its principal shrine at Dera Bába Nának in the Gurdaspur district. They pay special reverence to the *Adi Granth*, are generally celibate, and will eat food from any

* "Sákhi Sarwar is one of the only local Muhammadan Saints whom Sikhs do not ordinarily venerate and this because of the prohibition against the *jhatka* mentioned in the text."—Punjáb Ethnography.—*Densil Ibbetson.*

Hindu. Their service consists of a ringing of bells and blare of instruments, chanting of hymns and waving of lights before the *Adi Granth* and portrait of Nának. They are by no means uniform in their customs, some wear long hair, some short, and some wear caste marks, while others do not.

Udásis.

They generally burn their dead and subsist on voluntary offerings. In the Málwa districts the *Udásis* are mostly Jats by origin and are found in possession of the *Dharmsálas* where they distribute food to such as come for it, and read the *Granth*, both of Nának and Govind Singh. The head of each *Udási* brotherhood is called a *Mohant*, and his disciples *Chélas*. The ordinary dress of members of the sect is of a red colour, but many go entirely naked except for a waist cloth, and rub ashes all over their bodies. The majority are ascetics, but some engage in secular pursuits. *Udásis* are most numerous in the Jullundur, Rohtak, and Ferozepur districts, and number some 11,000 Sikhs.

The *Niranjani* fraternity was founded in the 16th century by Bába Handál, who was cook and tax-collector to Amar Dás, the third *Gúrú*, and worshipped the Almighty under the name of Niranjan or 'The Bright One.' His followers are styled *Niranjanis* or *Narinjanis*; they number about

Niranjanis.

3,000 and are found chiefly in the Jullundur, Amritsar, and Kapurthala districts. Their chief claim to notice is their rejection of the ordinary funeral customs of Sikhs and Hindus. They reject all *Kiria Karams* or funeral rites, and do not send the bones of their dead to the Ganges. They have special marriage rites of their own, and do not reverence Bráhmans. Their principal shrine is at Jandiála.

The *Rámráiás* number some 27,000 Sikh adherents and are found chiefly in Málwa. They are followers of Rám Rai, the elder brother of Gúrú Har Kishn, who was excluded from the office of *Gúrú* on account of his tendency to keep on good terms with the Mughal authorities, for which he was rewarded by a *jaghir* in the Dehra Dún. As the breach

Rámráiás.

between the Muhammadans and Sikhs widened, the relations of Rám Rai and his followers towards other Sikhs became more and more strained, and in the days of Govind Singh the mutual hatred of the two parties became very intense. The *Rámráias*, while acknowledging the other *Gúrús*, refused to recognize Gúrús Hargobind and Govind Singh; they follow the *Adi Granth*, and although they appear to lay some stress on the fact of their being Sikhs, they do not preserve the *khes* or long hair, and are expressly disclaimed by their orthodox *Khálsa* brethren. Members of his sect belong chiefly to the labouring and agricultural classes.

The *Nirmalas*, though *Govindi* Sikhs, have by degrees rid themselves of the main distinguishing marks of the *Khálsa* faith, and are gradually returning to a pure form of orthodox Hinduism. The *Nirmalas*, like the *Akális*, date from the time of Govind Singh. It is said that the *Gúrú* sent three followers to Benares to acquire a knowledge of Sanskrit, and that, on their return, he blessed them as being the only learned men among the Sikhs and called them *Nirmala*.* They were allowed to take the *pahúl* and founded the order of *Nirmala Sádhus*. The fraternity had at first great influence among the Sikhs, but their taste for Sanskrit literature led them to re-adopt many of the customs of the *Shástras*. They gave up the use of meat and spirits, and assumed the ordinary ochre-coloured dress of the Hindu *fakir* which is strictly prohibited to the true followers of Govind, and some of them are now only distinguishable from *Udásis* by wearing the *khes* or uncut hair. The headquarters of the sect are at Hardwár. They number about 3,000 and are found chiefly in the Gurdaspur, Umballa, Ferozepur, Amritsar, Patiála, and Faridkót districts. They are regarded as unorthodox by most classes of Sikhs, and are specially disliked by the *Akális*, with whom they have a standing quarrel with regard to the right to worship at the great Sikh shrine at Naderh or Abchalnagar in the Dekhan.

Nirmalas.

The *Akális* or *Nihangs* owe their origin to the express patronage of Gúrú Govind. The name means 'immortal', because they are followers of the *Akál Purkh* or 'Immortal God.' The generally received account of their origin is that Gúrú Govind, seeing his infant son playing before him with his turban peaked in the fashion now adopted by the *Akális*, blessed him and instituted a sect which should follow the same custom. The *Akális* first came into prominence during the reign of Ranjit Singh. Their headquarters were at Amritsar where they constituted themselves the guardians of the temple and the faith. They were the bravest and most unruly soldiers in the Sikh army, and their qualities were skilfully turned to account by Ranjit Singh, who employed them with success against his Pathán enemies across the Indus. The *Akáli* is distinguished very conspicuously by his dark blue dress and peaked turban which is often surmounted with steel quoits. He is most particular with regard to the five *kakkás*, and in preserving every outward form prescribed by Govind Singh. *Akális* do not eat meat or drink spirits, but are immoderate in the consumption of *bhang*. They are in other respects such purists that they will avoid Hindu rites even at their marriage ceremonies. The sect numbers some 1,500 adherents, and

Akális.

* The meaning of *Nirmalá* is 'spotless.'

is found chiefly in Amritsar and at Kiratpur in the Hoshiarpur district where there is a shrine to the memory of their leader Phula Singh.

Though the *Dévi Sikhs* are few in number and seldom enlisted, some mention must be made of this sect owing to the revival of Dévi-worship in the Punjáb where the goddess is said to have recently reappeared in the form of two little girls. They are found chiefly in Umballa and Hoshiarpur, and are regarded with some contempt by the stricter Sikhs of the central and western districts. Gúrú Govind Singh had in his youth a distinct bias towards Dévi-worship, probably owing the proximity of the great shrine of Naina Dévi to his home at Anandpur; but though the Dévi Sikh is thus historically connected with the early work of his *Gúrú*, he is now extremely lax in his religion, and has practically reverted to a superstitious and somewhat degraded type of Hinduism.

Dévi Sikhs.

We now come to what may be termed the modern forms of Sikh dissent. The first of these, a curious outcome of the *Udásis*, is the epicurian sect of *Gulábdásis* or *Sains*. An *Udási* fakir named Pritam Dás having received some slight at a great bathing festival on the Ganges, started this new sect, his principal disciple being a Jat Sikh named Gúlab Dás. The latter was a trooper in the service of Máhárája Sher Singh, and joined the sect on the collapse of the Sikh monarchy. He compiled a sacred book called the *Updes Bilás*, and taught that man is of the same substance as the Deity, with whom he will eventually be absorbed. They dispense with pilgrimages, the veneration of saints, and all religious ceremonies. Pleasure alone is their aim; and renouncing all higher objects they seek only for the gratificaiton of the senses, for costly dress and tobacco, wine and women, the lust of the eyes, and the pride of life. They are scrupulously neat in their attire and engage in all worldly pursuits, some of them being men of considerable wealth. They are said to have an especial abhorrence of lying, and there is certainly little or no hypocrisy in their tenets. In appearance they vary. Some always wear white clothes; others preserve the *Udási* dress; some are attired like *Nirmalas;* and others again are distinguished by always being shaved. They see no harm in incest, and have disgusted all respectable communities by their licence. The sect has only some 300 votaries, and is found chiefly in Lahore and Jullundur. All castes are admitted to the sect, but they do not eat with each other or intermarry.

Gulábdásis.

The *Nirankári* sect was founded by a Khatri of Peshawar named Bhai Diál Dás who settled in Ráwal Pindi about fifty years ago. He died there about 1870, and was succeeded in the office of *Gúrú* by his two sons. The word *Nirankar* means properly 'The Formless One' and was a term commonly used by Nának for describing the Deity. The *Nirankáris* worship God as a spirit only, avoid the adoration of idols, make no offerings to Bráhmans or to the dead, abstain strictly from flesh and wine, and are said to pay strict attention to the truth in all things. Their sacred book is the *Adi Granth* of Bába Nának. Their marriages are not performed according to the Hindu *Dharamshástras*, and the bride and bridegroom, instead of circumambulating the sacred fire, walk round a copy of the *Adi Granth*. The ceremony is conducted by a *Granthi* instead of a Bráhman, and widow marriage is not only allowed, but often takes place among them. At funerals they dispense with all Hindu ceremonials, and instead of mourning look upon death as an occasion for rejoicing. Besides the usual Sikh places of pilgrimage the *Nirankáris* look with special reverence upon a pool in the Park at Ráwal Pindi to which they have given the name of Amritsar. The sect is recruited from all castes and numbers some 38,000 Sikhs.

Nirankáris.

The most recent of the Sikh sects and the only one which has ever shown any active hostility to the British Government, is that of the *Kúkas* or 'Shouters,' founded by an *Udási* Aróra about the middle of the present century. His principal object appears to have been to break the power which the Bráhmans had acquired over the Sikhs. After his death the doctrines of the sect were disseminated by a carpenter named Rám Singh who proclaimed that he was an incarnation of Govind Singh, that the latter was the only true *Gúrú;* that no Bráhmans were ever to be employed; and that all worship save the reading of the *Granth* was prohibited. Establishing his headquarters at Baini in the Ludhiana district, disciples began to flock to him, and from the proceeds of their offerings he was able to erect a large *Dehra* and to travel about in considerable state. Early in 1872, a gang of his followers, after working themselves up into a state of religious frenzy, started off on a raid in the Patiala and Maler Kótla states. The state troops pursued and surrounded them after some desultory fighting in which several men were killed. Meanwhile British troops had been sent for, and on their arrival, forty-nine of the prisoners were blown away from guns under the orders of the Deputy Commissioner. Rám Singh was deported to Rangoon, where he died in 1887, being succeeded by his brother Budh Singh. The sect is known by the name of *Kúkas* or 'Shouters' because unlike ordinary Sikhs they permit themselves to fall into a state of frenzy during their religious exercises, shaking their heads and reciting their prayers in a loud voice. They finish their devotions with a loud cry of

Kúkas.

"*Sat Sri Akal*," "God is true," and their religious meetings are said to end sometimes in disgusting orgies. The *Kúkas* number some 10,000 Sikhs who will often try to conceal the fact of their belonging to this sect by calling themselves *Náindhdris.* They are found chiefly in the Jullundur, Ludhiána, Ferozepur, Patiála, Amritsar, Gújránwala and Sialkót districts. The true *Kúka* should carry a staff in his hand, tie his turban in a peculiar fashion called *sidha pag*, and wear a woollen necklace tied in knots. These signs, however, are falling into disuse; the straight *pagri* is often abandoned, and the necklace is worn under instead of over the clothing. *Kúkas* are supposed to avoid meat and spirits; many refuse to believe in the death of Rám Singh, and live in expectation of his early reappearance. In other respects they are only puritans of the school of Govind, with a more marked hatred of Muhammadans, butchers, and tobacco, than most other classes of Sikhs. The enlistment of *Kúkas* is strictly prohibited.

CUSTOMS.

The principal phases in the life of a Jat Sikh are celebrated by a number of ceremonies called *Karams*, of which only the more important need be mentioned, *viz.*, those relating to birth, baptism, marriage, and death. Needless to say the observance of these *Karams* is really a concession to Hinduism, and, as such, contrary to the Sikh religion; but the traditions of Bráhmanism are too strong to be ignored, and most Jat Sikhs find it convenient to conform in these matters to the customs of their Hindu neighbours.

CEREMONIES RELATING TO BIRTH.

About two months before the birth of the infant, the father informs his relations and friends of the expected event and fixes a day for their entertainment. Offerings are made to Bráhmans, presents of clothes and jewellery are made to the wife by her parents, and a gold or silver token called a *baranghári* is provided by a friend of the family to suspend round the infant's neck. The *dhai* or midwife is nearly always a woman of the Jhinwar, Dhánúk, or Chúhra caste. On the birth of the child the father distributes alms, and having prepared a small sweetmeat, places it in the infant's mouth.

Ját Karam or Birth.

If the latter is a boy, a *thali* or brass dish is generally beaten to apprise the neighbours, the representation of an outspread hand is made with a red dye on the outside walls of the house, and an iron ring and a branch of the *siris* tree are tied up over the doorpost.

The future destiny of the child is fixed on the eve of the sixth day after birth, and on it the women of the village come and sing, and the household passes the night in watching. The Bráhman who acts as *parohit* or domestic chaplain attends the father, and records the birth in the family books. A note of the event is also made by the local *Mirásis* and *Sánsis* who act as genealogists to the Jat *zámindars.*

A Jat mother is secluded for thirteen days after her confinement, and during this period lives with her child in a separate building, apart from the rest of the family. A cake of cowdung is kept burning in front of her door, night and day, in order to preserve the new-born infant from evil influences.

On the eve of the thirteenth day the females of the family *leep** the whole of the house, clothes are washed, all earthen vessels which have been used are broken, and all metal utensils are cleaned and scoured. On the day itself the *parohit* visits the household, lights the *hom* or sacred fire, and by way of purification sprinkles its members with Ganges water. The Bráhman, the Nai, and the relatives of the family are then feasted, and the father gives presents of clothes to his female kinsfolk; on the same day the various village menials bring the new-born infant toys typical of their various callings, and receive gifts from the parents in return.

When the new-born infant is a girl, formal congratulations are dispensed with, and the feasting and alms-giving, if not altogether omitted, are on a very much smaller scale.

Nam Karam or Naming.

On the 13th, 21st, and 41st day after birth the infant is taken to the *Granthi* or Sikh priest who after suitable prayers and thanksgivings bestows a name on the child. This is generally done by opening the *Granth* at haphazard. The first letter of the first line of the page at which the book opens, must be initial letter of the name bestowed on the infant. In some families the naming of the child is performed by a Bráhman instead of a *Granthi.* The former consults his *patra* or almanac and gives the father four names to choose from, each beginning with the same letter, claiming a small fee for his services.

BAPTISM OR INITIATION INTO THE SIKH RELIGION BY THE ADMINISTERING OF THE PAHUL.

Charan Ghâwal or Baptism.

The ceremony of baptism established by Nának for the initiation of his followers was called *Charan Ghâwal* and consisted in the drinking of water in which the feet of the *Gúrú* had been bathed. Though seldom used, it still exists

* The process called *leeping* consists of smearing the walls and floor with a mixture of mud and cowdung.

among the *Munnas and *Sajdhári* or *Nánakpanthi* Sikhs, who reverence Nának as their *Gúrú* in preference to Govind Singh.

Administering of the *pahúl* or Initiation. Sometimes called Amrita Diksha.

When a lad has reached a fairly intelligent age, say from twelve to eighteen, the *pahúl* is administered to him by the *Granthi*. Many of the recruits now enlisted do not actually take the *pahúl* until after they have joined their regiments. The neophyte is clothed with nothing but a turban and the *kachh*, a pair of short drawers reaching half way down to the knee. Some *amrit* or *sherbat** is sprinkled in his face and eyes, and the remainder he drinks from the palms of the hands, exclaiming "*Wah Gúrúji ka Khálsa, Wah Gúrúji ka Fatteh !*"

The *Granthi* then instructs him in the articles of his faith, and he is directed how to keep and care for his *khes*, and how to tie it into a *jurah* or top knot.

Five Sikhs must be present to make the initiation lawful, and the ceremony is concluded by all partaking of *kará parshád* or consecrated food which is distributed in equal proportions to *all* Sikhs present, irrespective of caste.

CEREMONIES RELATING TO MARRIAGE.

Age for betrothal.

The first great ceremony after birth and naming is *saggai* or betrothal. This among the higher classes takes place when the bride and bridegroom are from four to nine years old, but among the Jat peasantry it often takes place when the girl is ten, twelve, or even older, for the longer she is kept the higher the price she will fetch. Lads generally remain unmarried till eighteen or twenty, because their parents before then are unable to collect enough money to pay for a girl.† Marriage, under the circumstances, generally follows soon after betrothal.

One of the injunctions of Gúrú Govind to his followers was that no price should be taken by a Sikh for his daughter. Nevertheless the rule is more honoured in the breach than in the observance, for all Jats, with the exception of the highest families, have a custom, partly clandestine and partly recognized, under which money, varying in amount from Rs. 50 to Rs. 500, is paid for the girl to her parents. There are thus two forms of betrothal, one called *Pun*, of rare occurrence, in which the parents claim

---

* The *amrit* or *sherbat* consists of *patasa*, *i.e.*, sugar and water mixed in a stone bowl, and stirred by a two-edged dagger.

† Even to an ordinary cultivator a marriage in some parts often means an expenditure of from Rs. 500 to Rs. 1,000.

no price for their daughter, and the other, already described, in which a considerable sum is demanded. In united communities it is customary for a man's friends to contribute, each according to his means, towards the expenses of a marriage in his house, on the understanding that when they have the like need themselves, he shall contribute the same amount. Strict account is kept of these gifts, and the obligation to repay them, when opportunity arises, is held to be very stringent.

After selecting a propitious day, the father of the girl sends out his *Lagis* or matrimonial agents to some other village, to seek for a suitable bridegroom. The *Lagis* are generally three in number, one being a Bráhman, another a Nai, and the third a Mirási.* The *Lagis* select a candidate and having satisfied themselves as to his social position, the means of his parents, and his freedom from physical defects, return to their employer to report progress. If the latter is satisfied, and if he finds that his approaches are favourably received, he sends the Nai or Mirási to the lad's father with a sweetmeat and one rupee. The former is placed in the boy's mouth, the latter in his lap, and the Bráhman *padha* or *paróhit*, makes a red mark called a *tika* on his forehead. In the case of a betrothal for consideration, the parents of the girl generally receive a portion of their daughter's purchase money in advance, the actual marriage being deferred until after the payment of the balance. The ceremony is concluded by a feast given by the girl's relations, who are also expected to give presents to the *Lagis*. The investiture with the *tika* is generally confined to well-to-do families, and is accompanied in certain Jat clans by a very curious custom called *chédna*. The bridegroom cuts off a small piece from a ram's ear and rubs it on the cut until blood flows. He then places the piece in the centre of a *chapáti* with some rice, and smearing his thumb with the mixture, imprints a *tika* or mark on his own forehead.

Saggai or Betrothal, also called *Chuhara Karmai, Mangiah, or Lagan.*

On the termination of these rites, the *Lagis* return to their employer, taking with them a present of one rupee from the lad to his betrothed, and various other gifts such as rice, sugar, sweetmeats, a red *phulkári,* and some skeins of thread, etc. This formality called *Chuhára, Karmai, Mangiah,* or *Lagan,* completes the engagement, which may still however be cancelled if desired. The final ratification of the contract called *Ropna,*

*"The Mirasis are identical with the tribe known in some parts of India as Dums, and are descended from the Hindu Bháts, whose hereditary occupations they follow. They are the tribal bards and genealogists, and hold a recognised place among the village servants. Their duty is to know the traditions of the tribe they serve, the dates of its migrations, the places where it has sojourned, its different branches and families, with the roll of the ancestors of each subdivision. These multifarious details they master and retain, without the aid of writing, by dint of singularly retentive memories. They are also musicians and have a stock of ballads celebrating the exploits of the tribe."—The Punjábi Muhammadans.—*Boyle.*

may take place at any convenient time. The bridegroom's father sends the bride a gift of nine, eleven, or twenty-one rupees in cash, and various presents in kind. The girl keeps one rupee for herself, and the rest of the money is distributed by her father amongst his own *Lagis.* This formality makes the engagement binding on both parties.

Prohibited degrees.

Every Jat clan is exogamous, *i.e.*, while every man *must* marry into his own tribe no man *can* marry into his own clan, as such an union would be regarded as incest. Moreover no man can marry into any family of the *gots* to which his mother, or his paternal or maternal grandmothers belong. Besides the above prohibitions, it is unusual for a man to marry into a family of whatever clan it may be, that is settled in his own village, or in any village immediately adjoining his own. Unions between persons of different religion are forbidden, but for this purpose no difference is made between Jats who are Hindus and Jats who are Sikhs.

Age for marriage.

Marriage should take place in the first, third, or fifth year following betrothal. The even years are considered unlucky. In theory it is considered that a daughter should be married before she is twelve years of age,* but in most cases the services of a girl are so valuable to her family that she is detained by her father until she is fifteen, sixteen, or even older.

Beeáh, Shádi, Barát or Sart.

Beeah, *Shádi,* or marriage is the next step after *Saggai* or betrothal. The first thing to be done is to select an auspicious date for the ceremony. This, as a rule, involves numerous references to the stars, and every hitch in the proceedings has to be got over by propitiatory gifts to the *padhás* or *pundits.*

The most favourable season for marriages is the spring, but marriage may take place in any of the following months, each of which possesses peculiar attributes :—

Mágh, *i.e.*, from about	10th January	to 10th February.
Phágan, *i.e*, ,, ,,	10th February	to 10th March.
Baisákh, *i.e.*, ,, ,,	10th April	to 10th May.
Jéth, *i.e.*, ,, ,,	10th May	to 10th June.
Har or Asárh, *i.e.*, ,,	10th June	to 10th July.

The marriage season.

The month of *Mágh* is said to bring a wealthy wife; *Phágan* a good manager; *Baisákh* and *Jéth* a dutiful helpmate; while marriages in *Har* are reputed to be very prolific. No marriage should ever take place in the months of

*The pious Hindu believes that if his daughter grows up to puberty unmarried, several generations of his descendants will be damned. This obligation sits lightly upon the Sikh, but even he admits that an early marriage is more respectable.

Chét, Kartik, or Poh. About two months before the date fixed upon by the *pundits,* the parents of the bride give notice to the bridegroom's family that the marriage may take place on a certain day. This intimation is called the *Sahi chitthi* or 'marriage letter.' The document itself is called *Batar,* and is invariably sprinkled with saffron. It must be delivered to the lad's father by one of the *Lagis* not less than nine, and not more than twenty-one days before the actual date of the marriage.

The date of the ceremony being fixed,* invitations to the marriage feast are issued by the parents of both parties to their relations and friends, who are expected in their turn to make a collection in aid of expenses. Various rites and observances follow, such as the beating of drums, the rubbing of the bodies of bride and bridegroom with mustard oil, and the wearing of dirty clothes. To propitiate the stars, a Bráhman makes a square with some flour and divides it into nine portions to represent the nine Hindu planets, and worships the same in the name of bride and bridegroom. For these services he receives a fee from both their families. It is customary with most clans for the bridegroom to cut a twig of the *Jhand* tree before starting for the bride's village. This, combined with offerings to Bráhmans, is said to ensure a successful marriage. Another necessary observance is that the bridegroom should worship at the shrine of his *Jathera* or tribal ancestors.

The *Barát, Janét* or marriage procession.

On the morning of the bridegroom's departure for the bride's village, he is dressed in yellow, wreathed with a *séra* or necklace of flowers, and crowned with a *mukat* or headdress made of mica and tinsel paper, faced with a fringe of gold threads, as a screen from the evil eye. A Bráhman ties the *kangna,* or seven-knotted bracelet on the boy's wrist, and marshalled by the Nai, the *barát* or procession is ready to start. The bridegroom usually rides a mare, and at this point the bridegroom's sister seizes the reins as if to stop him, and usually demands a small present as an inducement to allow her brother to proceed. The *barát* is composed entirely of males, and as many of them as possible should be mounted. The procession should not reach the scene of the wedding before sunset, and on arrival halts in an open space outside the village called *khét* or *góra,* where the girl's relations come out to meet it with loud singing and beating of drums.

After dark, the bridegroom is conducted to the bride's house, surrounded by her friends and relations. The girl meanwhile is sometimes wrapped

* To postpone the date of the marriage after the *Sahi Chitthi* has been sent out, is considered a great disgrace, and generally results in the match being broken off besides causing considerable pecuniary loss.

in a blanket and passed five times under the belly and neck of his horse. The bridegroom then returns to his party, when carpets are spread and a feast takes place.

The same night, after the feast, the bridegroom again returns to the bride's house. The young couple are seated on stools, facing east, the girl being placed on the left; a fire is kindled before them, and a red *phulkári* called *bédi*, is spread as a canopy over the whole. A Bráhman then ties the hem of the girl's *chadar* to a piece of cloth. The bridegroom takes the latter over his shoulder, and guided by a relative leads her four times round the *agni* or sacred fire which is supposed to be a witness of the ceremony. The bride then comes to the front and three more circuits are made, the bride leading her husband, while the *pundits* chant prayers, and recite *mántras* or texts from the *Shástras.** The girl is meanwhile carefully muffled up in a wrap, grains of barley are thrown over the young couple, and mutual promises are exchanged. The hand of the bride is then given to the bridegroom by her nearest male relation, and sweetmeats are placed by her mother in each of their mouths. The ceremony being thus completed amidst general rejoicings, the young couple separate for the night.

Phéra, Beeáh or Láwan.

This constitutes the *Phéra* or real marriage. It is then, for the first time, that the bride dons a small gold nose-ring and substitutes at least five glass wristlets on each wrist in place of the silver ones hitherto worn. These form her *sohág*, and a woman who has a husband living must always wear them. Loud singing and beating of drums accompanies almost every portion of the marriage service, as a curious idea prevails that the efficacy of all religious rites is greatly enhanced by noise.

The day following the marriage is spent in feasting, rejoicing, settling the dowry accounts, and observing the ceremonies which precede the departure of the bride. The young couple are seated on a bed, the bridegroom at the head and the bride at the foot. A little water is placed in the palm of the bridegroom's hand and sprinkled around the bed by the bride's parents. After this the girl is seated in a dooly and, accompanied by her *Lagis* and the Nai's wife, sets out for her husband's house. Here she makes a stay of forty days, and then returns to her own home, where she remains until old enough to cohabit with her husband.

Gáona, *Mukláwa*, or home-taking.

The last of the ceremonies relating to marriage is *Gáona*, also called *Mukláwa* or home-taking. This usually takes place when the bridegroom is about fifteen

* As has before been explained, Sikhs, like Hindus, nearly all employ Bráhmans at their weddings. In the case of an orthodox Singh family, however, the *Granth* takes the place of the *Shástras*, and a *Granthi* officiates in lieu of the *Pundit*.

or sixteen and the girl about twelve. A propitious day is selected, in consultation with the *parohit*, and the husband then pays a short visit to his wife's family, which is made the occasion for more ceremonies accompanied by rejoicing and feasting. The final leave is then taken, and the young people start for home, this time to commence life together in earnest. If unavoidable circumstances prevent the bridegroom from attending, the bride may be taken home by her father-in-law or her husband's brother. Owing to the fact that marriages among Jats are frequently deferred until both parties are fully grown up, the *Mukláwa* or consummation often takes place at the same time as the *Phéra*. In this case the bride stays for three days with her husband, and then returns to her father's house, where she remains until sent for by her husband.

According to the *Dhárma Shástras* on a man dying and leaving no male heir, the widow inherits the estate. But in wild times when the sword was the only arbiter in disputes, and women were too weak to hold what had been won by the strength of men, the practice had great inconveniences. The Sikh women showed themselves in many instances the equals of their brothers in wisdom and administrative ability; but, as a rule, an estate which fell into the hands of a Sikh widow was apt to be exploited by her lover, till it would be seized by some one stronger, and with as valid a claim to its possession. To avert this evil, and to avoid the many disputes which it caused between the widow and the nephews and brothers of the deceased, the practice followed by the Jews* in Biblical times, of marriage with a brother of the late husband, was introduced. The widow was generally allowed a choice between the brothers, but with the elder lay the right if he chose to exercise it. This form of marriage is known as *chadar dálna* ;† also as *karáo* or *karewa*.‡ It has the double advantage of perpetuating the deceased brother's name and of being economical, for when the eldest son of a Jat dies, the latter utilises the piece of female property § left on his hands by bestowing his widowed daughter-in-law on any of his sons unprovided with a wife. As the origin of the practice was to secure

Karao, Karewa. Chadar dalna, or widow marriage.

the succession in the family, the offspring of these unions were considered quite as legitimate as those of the more formal *shádi* or *beeáh*, and enjoyed the same right to inheritance; but as a matter of precedence and dignity, they were not held in equal honour. The convenience of the *chadar dálna* marriage, especially in time of war when the elaborated ceremony of the *beeáh* was

* Deuteronomy XXV, verse 5.

† *Chadar dálna* signifies 'throwing the sheet.'

‡ *Karáo* or *karéwa* is derived from *kari hui, i. e.*, a woman who has been married.

§ *Mal* is the term actually used for describing a bride for whom a dowry has been paid.

impossible or unsuited to the rank or caste of the bride who might be a slave girl or a captive, caused its general extension to other unions than those with the brother's widow. It is thus possible for a Jat or Sikh to marry a widow whom he could not have married as a virgin, the only restriction being that she should not be of his own *gót* or sept. A *karáo* marriage must not take place until a year after widowhood. It is effected by the man throwing a red *chadar* or wrap over the woman's head and putting *chura* or wristlets over her arms in presence of the male and female members of the brotherhood. The ceremony is generally known as *chadar dálna.* It is unaccompanied by rejoicings of any kind, the woman merely resuming her jewels and the coloured clothes which she ceased to wear on her first husband's death. Where children have been born to the deceased husband, *karéwa* seldom takes place. The right of the widow to remarry at her own choice when she is not claimed by her late husband's brother is universally admitted, and there are instances of women making even third marriages called *thréwa.* The tendency of modern Sikhism, however, is to conform, especially in matters of this kind, to the ordinary usages of Hindus; widow marriages, therefore, except the *Karéwa* unions above described, must be rare in the present day.

CEREMONIES RELATING TO DEATH.

When death is approaching, a *Pundit* or *Granthi* is sent for. The sick man is placed with his bedding on the ground, on a spot which has previously been leeped or enclosed in a ring of cowdung.* A sprig of the *túlsi* plant and a few drops of Ganges water (of which a little is kept in every house) are placed in his mouth. The object of these precautions is to detain Yáma, the God of Death, until the proper propitiatory ceremonies have been carried out. A light is then placed in the dying person's hand, to light his way on his gloomy journey through the world of shades.†

After death, the *Mahá-Bráhman* or *Acháraj*, a despised individual specially entrusted with the performance of funeral rites, makes a ball or *pinda* of flour which is offered to the deceased while the body is covered with a white cloth. The corpse is then conveyed to the burning place, which is generally on the bank of a stream or tank, on a wooden bier called a *sirhi*,‡ carried by four men. When the funeral procession reaches

* A person dying in an unorthodox manner is said to have died *avghat*, *i. e.*, not on the ground, and is supposed to become a *bhút* or malevolent spirit.

† Needless to say many of these ceremonies would, under ordinary circumstances, be dispensed with. In this, as in most things, the difference between theory and practice is very marked.

‡ Among Sikhs a charpoy should never be used as a bier.

halfway, water is sprinkled in a circle round the bier, and the son or nearest relative dashes an earthen vessel on the ground and bewails the deceased. If the latter, however, was an elderly person, a brass vessel is thrown down in lieu of an earthen one, and instead of mourning there is general rejoicing. On reaching the burning *ghát*, a pile is erected, on which the body is laid, generally facing north. Five *pindas* or balls of rice are placed on the body, and the heir, taking some sacred fire lit by a Bráhman, lights the wood of the pyre, and fans it. While the body is being consumed the relations sit around at some distance, and when it is partly burnt, the eldest son or next-of-kin takes one of the sticks of which the bier was composed and breaks the skull. This is supposed to facilitate the escape of the soul from the body. When the cremation is over, all bathe before returning to their homes. The burning should be on the day of death if possible, and always before sunset. The bones that remain unburnt, called *phul*, or *ast*, are collected on the third or fourth day after the cremation.

It is a favourite act of filial piety to take the *phul* to the Ganges, and if the heir is well-to-do, he will almost certainly build a mausoleum or *chhatri* over the spot where his relative's remains were burnt.*

If a man dies in a remote place, or if his body is not found, his son should make an effigy of the deceased with *khúsa* grass, and then burn it on a pile with similar rites. This procedure is very generally observed by the relations of sepoys who die on service or abroad.

Period of mourning.

The period of mourning is three days for ordinary relatives and eleven days for the son or other relation who performs the funeral obsequies. On the thirteenth day the *Achára j* is sent for, and if the deceased was a male, receives as his perquisite an umbrella, a stick, a pair of shoes, a turban, also the deceased's charpoy, wearing apparel, and often a little opium. If the deceased was a woman, he is generally given some articles of female clothing. Should the deceased have met with a violent death, such as by drowning, hanging, poisoning, or snake-bite, or if he or she died prior to being lifted off the bed on to the ground, the relatives repair to certain shrines in the Umballa district called Kurkhetar and Pahoya, and there offer up prayers for the salvation and redemption of the deceased.

On the eleventh day after death, the *Dharm Shant*, *Kanágat*, or *Shráddha*† ceremonies commence. These are reverential offerings to

* If it is not convenient to take the *phul* to the Ganges, they may, after making suitable offerings at the Akál Bungah, be ground to powder and scattered in the *chaugird* or promenade of the *Darbar Sahib* at Amritsar, or of one of the other *Gurdwáras*.

† The *Shráddha* ceremonies are contrary to the Sikh religion, for one of Govind Singh's ordinances was that "he who worships graves and dead men is no Sikh." Nevertheless in this, as in many other matters affecting social life, Hindu custom is generally adhered to.

ancestral spirits. *Pindas* of rice, *ghi*, and sugar are scattered about, and a vessel of water is hung on a *pipal* tree, for the use of the soul of the deceased until its final departure for another world, which is supposed to take place on the thirteenth day. On the seventeenth day the mourning is over, friends, kinsmen, and an *odd* number* of Bráhmans must be fed, walls must be plastered, earthern vessels changed, and clothes washed in order that the house may be pure.

The *Shráddha* ceremonies are repeated in a simple form every month for one year, and afterwards twice a year—on the anniversary of the death, and again in the month of September. On the fourth anniversary called *Chaubarsi*, the chief mourner gives a cow and some clothes to a Bráhman. There are certain occasions when Jats and Sikhs forego the observance of these rites. Thus the bodies of very young children are sometimes buried instead of being burnt, generally in the *angan* or courtyard of the father's house.

LEAVE.

The amount of leave required by a sepoy or sowár to enable him to take part in any of the ceremonies previously described, will depend upon the distance at which he is quartered from his home, and the proximity of the latter to a railway. The number of days granted must be sufficient to cover the time spent in travelling to and fro, in addition to the minimum period required for each rite, which is generally as follows:—

	Days.
(*a*) *Jat Karam* (birth); *Nám Karam* (naming) ...	3
(*b*) *Barát, Beeáh or Phéra* (marriage) ...	10

When granting leave for this ceremony, consideration must be taken of the distance of the bridegroom's house from that of the bride. Allowing for a stay of four days, and six days for the journey there and back, ten days' leave will as a rule be ample.

	Days.
(*a*) *Gáona* or *Muklâwa* (home-taking) ...	10
(*b*) *Kiria Karams* (funeral rites)	17

The period of leave should be reckoned from the date of death.

SIKH AND HINDU FESTIVALS, FAIRS, AND PLACES OF PILGRIMAGE.

The number of purely Sikh festivals and fairs is comparatively small, but owing to the tendency of Sikhism to conform in matters of this kind to ordinary Hindu usage, it has been considered advisable to give a short account of all the more important religious festivals observed by the Hindu races of the Punjáb. The list, however, is necessarily incomplete, for nearly every district has local festivals of its own. A schedule of gazetted holidays is

* It is customary to feed an *even* number of Bráhmans at times of rejoicing, such as births, marriages, etc., and an *odd* number on occasions of grief or mourning.

published annually by the Punjáb Government, copies of which may be obtained for regimental reference on application to the Civil authorities.

Name of festival.	Month in which it usually falls.	Remarks.
Makar Sankránt ...	January ...	The celestial sign Makar answers to *Capricorn*. On that day the sun is said to begin his journey northward. To the early Aryans, living in a cold region, the approach of spring was an occasion of the greatest joy, and the commencement of the sun's northward progress could not pass unmarked, for then opened the auspicious half of the year. The sun especially is worshipped at this festival. Bathing in the sea is prescribed whenever it is possible. Rejoicings abound in public and in private. Great gatherings take place at Allahabad, where the Ganges and Jumna mingle; also at Ganga-Ságar, where the Ganges meets the ocean. Among Sikhs the festival is observed by a great fair at Mukatsar in the Ferozepur district, which lasts three days. The worshippers bathe in the sacred tank and repair to the *Tibbi Sáhib* or holy mound where Gúrú Govind Singh stood and discharged his arrows against the imperial forces. The festival among Sikhs commemorates a battle fought in 1705 between Gúrú Govind and the Mughals who overtook him at Mukatsar and cut his followers to pieces. The *Gúrú* himself escaped and had the bodies of his retainers burned with the usual rites. He declared that they had all obtained *mukhti, i.e.*, the final emancipation of their souls from the ills of transmigration, and promised the same blessing to all his followers who should thereafter bathe in the Holy Pool, which had been filled by rain from heaven in answer to his prayer for water. On the spot a fine tank was afterwards dug by Ranjit Singh, and called *muktisáras*, 'the pool of salvation,' a word which was afterwards contracted into *mukatsar*, the present name of the place.
Mauni Amáwas ...	January-February...	A minor holiday. Persons observing this festival do not speak to any one until they have performed the ablutions prescribed for the occasion. Bathing may take place in the nearest large river or tank, but, if possible, it should be carried out in the Ganges or Jumna, and especially at Hardwár.

Name of festival.	Month in which it usually falls.	Remarks.
Bhaibála or Bhaiwála	January-February ...	This is a local festival of the Ludhiána district held in honour of a disciple of Gúrú Nának called Bála. There is a shrine and tank where Sikhs and Hindus make offerings of grain, money, etc., which are taken by the *massands* or guardians. Pilgrims make curds overnight and eat or distribute them after presentation to the shrine. With a view to increasing the size of the tank, it is the duty of every devotee to scoop out some handfuls of earth.
Basant Panchmi ...	January-February ...	A spring festival. In Bengal, Sáraswáti, goddess of arts and learning, is worshipped at this time. No reading or writing is permissible, and the day is observed as a holiday in all public offices. Both sexes should wear *basanti* or yellow clothing, and celebrate the festival with music and rejoicings. From the fact that the festival takes place about the time that the yellow leaves of the mustard plant are in bloom, it is customary among the Sikhs and Hindus of the Punjáb to wear mustard seed in their turbans in token of the day.
Sheorátri, properly Máha-Sivá-rati, the great night of Siva.	February-March ...	Commemorates the birth of Siva. A fast is observed during the day, and a vigil is kept at night, when the *linga* or phallus is worshipped in the *Shiválas* or temples of Siva.
Holi	February-March ...	This festival, identified with *dola-yatra*, or the rocking of the image of Krishna, is celebrated, especially in Hindústán and the Punjáb, as a kind of Hindu Saturnalia or Carnival. Boys dance about the streets, and inhabitants of houses sprinkle the passer-by with red powder, use squirts, and play practical jokes, Towards the close of the festival, about

Name of festival.	Month in which it usually falls.	Remarks.
		the night of full moon, a bonfire is lighted, and games, representing the frolics of the young Krishna, take place around the expiring embers. During the Holi women are addressed with the utmost familiarity, and indecent jests at their expense are considered permissible. Among Sikhs, the Holi is celebrated by great fairs, held chiefly at Anandpur and Kiratpur in the Hoshiarpur district. The *Gúrúdwáras* or Sikh shrines are visited by the pilgrims, and offerings are made which are taken by the attendants. Of these shrines the most popular are the *Gúrúdwára Khesgarh* where Gúrú Govind Singh administered the *pahúl* to his first five disciples, and the *Gúrúdwára Anandpur Sáhib* which is said to mark the site of the Gúrú's own house. The Holi fair at Anandpur lasts two days, and on the afternoon of the second day the devotees of the various shrines bring out from each its particular standard, which they carry with singing and music to the neighbouring *Chokh.* The processions of priests and worshippers, clustering round their respective standards, move slowly about, accepting offerings and bestowing blessings on the people. Immediately preceding this fair, large numbers of persons visit the shrines at Kiratpur. The most important of the latter is that sacred to Bába Gurditta, son of Hargovind, and father of Har Rai, the sixth and seventh Gúrús. Considerable offerings both of cash and sweetmeats are made at this shrine. The food is distributed to all Sikhs present and the cash appropriated by the two principal *Sódhis.**
Rám Naumi ...	March-April ...	This is commemorative of the birthday of Ráma. It is kept as a strict fast. The temples of Ráma are illuminated, and his image adorned with costly ornaments. The *Rámayana* is read in the temples and nautches are kept up during the night. At noon of this day the *pujári* (*i.e.,* the Bráhman who conducts worship at a temple) exhibits a small image of the god and puts it into a cradle. The assembly prostrates itself

* The Granthis or priests of the Sikhs (except Mazbhi Sikhs) all belong to the Khatri caste and the most influential families among them are those that belong to the *Sodhi* and *Bedi* subdivisions, Bába Nának was a *Bedi*, but all the Gúrús from Rám Dás onwards were of the *Sodhi* clan.

Name of festival.	Month in which it usually falls.	Remarks.
		before it. Acclamations arise all round; handfuls of red powder are flung in token of joy; and all go home exulting.
Sákhi Sarwar ...	March-April ...	The shrine of Sákhi Sarwar near Dehra Ghazi Khan is a favourite place of pilgrimage for Sultáni Jats. They march from their homes in large bodies in the month of March and return in April. A visit to this shrine is said to cure leprosy, and to secure for the pilgrim all he wishes. A fair is held annually in February in honour of Sarwar at Lahore.
Worship of the Sutlej, and Sárústi or Sáraswáti.	March-April ...	The great festival for the worship of the Sutlej takes places at Pehowar and at Rupar in the Umballa district, where large crowds assembled early in April to reverence the river at the spot where it issues from the hills. The attendance of visitors to shrines at Thanesar and other places on the Sarusti goes on throughout the year, more especially on occasions of eclipses of the sun.
Rájni Dévi ...	March-April ...	The shrines of Dévi, the small-pox goddess, in the Hoshiarpur district, are largely patronised by the Mánjha Sikhs who make their offerings every Tuesday during the month of *Chéth.* The Málwa Sikhs pay equal reverence to the shrine at Manimajra in Umballa, where Dévi is worshipped as the patron saint of thieves and cattle lifters.
Panjgátra. The name is derived from the five stones said to have been used by the sons of the *Pándus* in the game of *Pánch Satara.*	April-May ...	The festival is held at Babhaur on the Sutlej, in which the pilgrims bathe in large numbers. Brámawati, as this part of the Sutlej is called, is held to be very sacred, especially since 1895, when the Ganges, except at Hardwar, lost something of its sacred character.
Baisákhi ...	April-May ...	This is primarily a Sikh religious festival held at Amritsar, but the meetings have gradually come to be utilized for the buying and selling of cattle. On these occasions all the *bhungas* or hospices originally kept up by leading families round the Tank of the *Darbar Sáhib* or Golden Temple, and all the semi-religious

Name of festival.	Month in which it usually falls.	Remarks.
		Akhdras or rest-houses, are filled to overflowing with representatives of every race in the Punjáb. The *Baisákhi Amáwas* is also called *Satudhi Amáwas* because it is customary to make offerings of *Sattu* or ground barley and gram to Bráhmans during the festival.
Dasehra-Jeth ...	May-June ...	Commemorates the birthday of Gunga, goddess of the Ganges. On this day, all Hindus who are able to do so, bathe in the Ganges, and give alms to the Bráhmans living on its bank. By so doing they secure the benefits of *dasehra*, *i.e.*, ten-removing sins—an attribute of the goddess Gunga "who effaces ten sins, however heinous, of such as bathe in her holy waters."
Káli Dévi ...	May-June ...	The shrine of the goddess is at Niazbeg near Lahore. She is supposed to be potent for good and evil. Votive offerings are constantly placed on her shrines, especially by women, who pray to her for the fulfilment of their wishes. The fair to Káli Dévi is largely frequented by Sikhs from Lahore and Amritsar.
Nág-Panchmi ...	July-August ...	The festival is in honour of the Nágas or snake-gods. The figure of a serpent is made of clay, or drawn on the wall, and worshipped. Living serpents are brought and fed with milk and eggs. All this is done in order to deprecate the wrath of the venomous reptile.
Sitála-Saptami, or Sil, or Sile.	July-August ...	A minor festival observed in honour of *Sitála* and her seven sisters, who are supposed to cause small-pox and other pustular diseases. The goddess is also known as Masáni, Basanti, Máha Mai, etc., and is worshipped every Monday. The temple of Masáni at Gurgaon is a favourite shrine visited chiefly in April or May.
Raksha-Bandhah ...	July-August ...	A minor Hindu festival on which Bráhmans invoke protection for their clients, against all evils during the coming year by binding coloured thread or silk round their wrists.

Name of festival.	Month in which it usually falls.	Remarks.
Janam-Ashtmi, properly Krishna Janam-Ashtmi.	July-August ...	Celebrates the birth of Krishna. It is one of the greatest of the sacred seasons. The worshippers fast the whole day. At night they bathe, worship a clay image of the infant Krishna and adorn it with flowers and leaves of the *túlsi* plant. Next day is a great festival for keepers of cattle as Krishna spent his boyhood among cowherds.
Ganésh-Chattúrthi ...	August-September...	A minor festival in commemoration of the birthday of Ganésh, god of wisdom. Clay figures of the deity are made, and after being worshipped for a few days, are thrown into the water.
Anant-Chaudas ...	August-September...	Commemorates the commencement of the winter season.
Pit-Páksh, properly Pitri-Páksha or the fortnight of the Pitris or divine fathers; also called Mahalíya Amáwas.	September ...	This name is applied to the sixteen consecutive lunar days which are devoted to the performance of the *Shráddha* or *Kandgat* ceremonies in honour of ancestors and deceased relatives. Among Málwa Sikhs when anyone dies an unnatural death, such as by an accident, snake-bite, etc., the funeral obsequies have to be performed by the Bráhmans of Pihewa in the Umballa district. There is therefore a constant stream of Sikh and Hindu pilgrims to this place.
Gúga Pír or Zahir Pír ka púja.	August-September and every Monday throughout the year.	Gúga Pír, though a Muhammadan, is supposed to be the greatest of the snake-kings. His principle shrine is near Hissar. The efficacy of prayers to this saint in cases of snake-bite is much believed in. He is associated by the people with the Panj Pír or five Pandu brothers. A great fair is held annually at Chapár in the Ludhiana district in honour of this saint. Offerings are made at his *mori* or shrine where cattle are brought to be blessed.
Dévata or Nágan ka púja.	August-September ...	These are female snake deities, known by the people as Singhs. They are always distinguished by some colour and are most commonly worshipped as Káli, Hari, and Bhuri Singh, or black, green, and brown. Most villages have shrines

Name of festival.	Month in which it usually falls.	Remarks.
		devoted to them. They cause fever, but are not on the whole very malevolent. They have great power over milch cattle and are fond of offerings of milk. They are connected in the minds of the people with their *pitr* or ancestors, though it is difficult to see where the connection lies. Wherever the worship of *pitrs* is most prevalent, there the snake-gods are especially reverenced.
Dasehra Naorátri, Dúrga-Púja, or Rám-Lila.	September-October	This is the longest and most important of all Hindu festivals. It lasts ten days. It is celebrated all over India, and is connected with the autumn equinox. It nominally commemorates the victory of Dúrga or Káli, wife of Siva, over a buffalo-headed demon. The form under which she is adored is that of an image with ten arms and a weapon in each hand, her right leg resting on a lion, and her left on the buffalo demon. This image is worshipped daily until the end of the festival, when it is cast into a river. The fourth is the sacrificial day, on which buffaloes, male-goats and sheep are decapitated before the idol, to which the heads and blood of the victims are presented as offerings. The tenth day is called *Dasa-hara* or *Dasehra*. In Upper India and the Punjáb the *Ram-Lila* or sports of Ráma take place on the same day as the *Dúrga-Púja* in Bengal. They commemorate the victory gained by Ráma over Ravana, king of Ceylon. A pageant is gone through consisting of an out-door theatrical representation of the storming of Ravana's castle. Conspicuous in the midst of the fortress is the giant himself, a huge figure with many arms, each grasping a weapon, and bristling with fireworks. Besides him sits Sita, the wife of Ráma, whom the giant has abducted. Without stands the indignant Rama, demanding restitution of his wife, which being refused, the besiegers advance to the attack. Conspicuous among the assailants is Hanuman with his army of men dressed up as monkeys. The assault is at first repulsed, but is speedily renewed, this time with success. Sita is rescued, and Ravana is on the point of being captured when he blows up, thus finishing a *tamásha* which is much appreciated by natives of every creed.

Name of festival.	Month in which it usually falls.	Remarks.
Déo-uthán-Ekadasi or Deváthri.	October-November	This festival commemorates the awaking of Vishnu from four months' sleep. The image of the god is placed on a chair and rocked.
Diwáli or the feast of lamps. Also calléd Diwah.	October-November	Commemorates the birth of Lakshmi, wife of Vishnu, goddess of wealth and fortune. Houses are freshly *leeped*, whitewashed, and illuminated. Gambling is permitted, almost enjoined during the feast. Fireworks are displayed. The Banyas and traders close their accounts for the year, and get new ledgers and books, which are consecrated and then worshipped. It is the Hindu New Year's Day. Thieves are particularly active during this festival; they consider a successful robbery committed then to be very auspicious, and to promise good luck during the year just commenced. The festival is celebrated by a great fair held at Amritsar which is largely attended by Sikhs.
Gunga-Asnán ...	November ...	The great festival of the Ganges, held in honour of Siva's victory over the demon Tripurasura. Large gatherings take place at Gurmuktesar, Bithur, Allahabad, Sonepur and other places. All should bathe in the Ganges or some sacred river. The great *Kumbh* festival in honour of the Ganges takes place at Hardwar once in every twelve years.
Gúrú Nának's Birthday.	November ...	Bába Nának, the founder of the Sikh religion, was born at Talwandi or Nankana near Lahore where a fair is held annually in his honour.
Sómwári-Amáwas ...	Any month ...	The fifteenth of any Hindu month falling on a Monday. It is observed as a religious festival for bathing and giving alms.
Súraj-Girhan ...	Any month ...	A day on which a solar eclipse occurs.
Chandar-Girhan ...	Any month ...	A day on which a lunar eclipse occurs.

Name of festival.	Month in which it usually falls.	Remarks.
Bhúmiya or Jathéra-ka púja.	15th day of the month, every Sunday, and at births and marriages.	These days are specially devoted to the worship of the *Bhúmiya* or local village deity and the *Jathéra* or tribal ancestor whose shrine is generally a little masonry platform or a mound of earth under a *pipal* tree. One of the most celebrated of these *Jathéras* is Kála Mahar, the ancestor of the *Sindhu* Jats, who has peculiar influence over cows and to whom the first milk of every cow is offered.
Khwája Khizr ka Púja.	After each harvest and on Sundays.	In the Eastern Punjáb Khwája Khizr is the god of water, though the name really belongs to one of the Muhammadan prophets whose duty it is to look after travellers. Twice a year after he harvests he is worshipped at the well, lamps being lighted and Bráhmans fed. At the *Diwáli* and *Holi* festivals a tiny raft is made of grass, and a lamp put on it, which is launched and set afloat on the village tank in his honour.

In addition to the above it is customary to celebrate the birthdays and deathdays of all the *Gúrús*.

PLACES OF PILGRIMAGE.

The chief shrines of the Sikhs are at Amritsar, Patna, Naderh, Taran Taran, Mukatsar, Kartapur and Panja Shah The sanctity of Amritsar and Naderh have already been described. Patna is held to be sacred as it was the birth place of Gúrú Govind. Taran Taran is famous for its tank, the waters of which are said to cure leprosy. Panj Shah near Rawal Pindi, is celebrated as the place where Gúrú Nának performed some extraordinary miracles,

CHAPTER IV.

CHARACTERISTICS.

Influence of the Jats in forming the national character of the Sikhs.

Sikhism, as has already been explained, originated in a religious movement which drew its adherents from all classes, each of which possessed distinctive manners and customs; the social and numerical preponderance of the Jats, however, carried such weight in the formation of the national character, that the customs of the Sikh, whatever his origin, may now be considered as practically identical with those of the Punjáb Jat.

The Jat of the Punjáb.

The Jats of the Punjáb, whether Sikh or Hindu, are in every respect the most important of the Punjáb races. In point of numbers, the Jat surpasses the Rájpút, who comes next to him in the proportion of one to three. Politically he ruled the Punjáb till the *Khálsa* yielded to the British arms; "ethnologically he is the peculiar and most prominent product of the plains of the five rivers; while, from an economical and administrative point of view, he is *par excellence* the husbandman, the peasant, and the revenue payer of the province." His manners indeed do not bear that impress of generations of wild freedom which marks the races of Afghán hills, but he is more honest, more industrious, and at least their equal in courage and manliness."

General characteristics.

Sturdy independence, and patient vigorous labour, are perhaps the strongest characteristics of the Jat Sikhs. In certain tracts, where the Jats have the field to themselves, and are compelled, in default of rivals of other castes, to fall back upon each other for somebody to quarrel with, tribal ties are strong. "But as a rule the Jat is a man who does what seems good in his own eyes and sometimes what is wrong also, and will not be said nay by any man. He is far from turbulent, but is independent and self-willed. He is usually content to cultivate his fields in quietness if people will leave him alone, though when he does go wrong he takes to anything from gambling to murder, with perhaps a preference for abducting his neighbours' wives and carrying off their cattle."* Although ready to fight on occasion, he is not of a cruel or vindictive disposition, but always asserts personal

* Ethnography of the Punjáb.—*Denzil Ibbetson.*

freedom, as against communal or tribal control, more strongly than any other class.

The Jat as an agriculturist.

In agriculture the Jat Sikh is pre-eminent. No one can rival him as a landowner and yeoman cultivator. He calls himself a *zamindár* or husbandman as often as a Jat, and his women and children work with him in the fields. Indeed, it is a common saying in the Punjab that "the Jat's baby has a ploughandle for a plaything." Among the higher classes of Jat Sikhs, the women do not perform the harder descriptions of field-work as is the custom among their Hindu brethren; nevertheless they assist their husbands in various ways, and thus form a marked contrast to Rájpút and Muhammadan females who, being secluded, are lost to agricultural labour.

Condition of the people.

Taken as a whole, the Jat Sikhs are comfortably off. Almost all their villages have a prosperous air, and give evidence of the owners having a very fair standard of comfort. Well-kept *dharmsálas** and well-built drinking wells are seen in almost every district, the peasants are well-clothed, and, judging from their physique, well and sufficiently fed. Canal irrigation and the export of wheat have done much to enrich the people, but they are apt to squander much of their wealth in costly litigation, and in the extravagant observance of marriages and religious festivals.

Disposition of the Jat Sikh.

It has been truly said of the Jat Sikhs that "they are manly without false pride; undemonstrative; independent without insolence; reserved in manner, but good-natured, light-hearted, and industrious. No one could be associated with them for any time without conceiving both respect and liking for them."† These qualities, however, are differently impressed upon different races and localities. Thus "the Jat of the Mánjha is conspicuously genial and good-tempered, joining heartily in games and recreations, while the Málwai, if less genial, is more stubborn, and works quite as conscientiously but less cheerfully; this very stolidity renders him perhaps less liable to panic, and though the Mánjha Sikh was preferred by Ranjit Singh to his *confrère* from the Málwa, there is really very little to choose between them."‡ Some of the proverbs§ of the Punjáb would lead one to suppose that the Jat is not very

* *Dharmsála* is a village rest-house and place of prayer.

† Despatches regarding the Delhi Territories.—*Thomason.*

‡ Memorandum on Sikhs.—*Rice.*

§ The following sayings of the Punjáb peasants are typical of their jealousy of the Jats :—" The Jat, the Bhát, the caterpillar, and a widow woman, these four are best hungry ; if they eat their full they do harm." " The soil, fodder, clothes, hemp, múnj grass and silk, these six are best when beaten, and the seventh is the Jat."

popular with his neighbours, but this disfavour may be attributed to the jealousy of weaker and less industrious races, envious of the prosperity of their Jat rivals. The typical Jat Sikh is faithful and true to his employer, seldom shows insubordination, and with a good deal of self-esteem has a higher standard of honour than is common among most Orientals.

Social position of the Jat in relation to other classes.

Among races of purely Hindu origin, the Jat stands next after the Bráhman, the Rájpút, and the Khatri. He is of course below the Rájpút, for the simple reason that he practices *karáo* or widow-marriage, but he stands first among the classes in which this custom is permissible. "The Baniya with his sacred thread, his strict Hindúism, and his twice-born standing, looks down on the Jat as a Súdra,* but the Jat looks down on the Baniya as a cowardly spiritless money-grubber, and society in general agrees with the judgment of the Jat." The position of the Jat Sikh, however, is considerably higher than that of his Hindu *confrère.* This may be attributed partly to the fact that he is a soldier as well as an agriculturist, and partly to the freedom and boldness which he has inherited from the traditions of the *Khálsa.* The haughty Rájpúts who, according to Hindu ideas, are the natural leaders of society, were offended by the democratic ideas of Gúrú Govind, and declined to join his standard. They soon paid the penalty of their pride. The Jats who composed the great mass of the *Khálsa* rose to absolute power, and the Rájpúts, who had formerly despised them, became the peculiar objects of their hatred and oppression. As the Sikhs became the dominant, landowning, and military class of the Punjáb, they gradually acquired the social position usually accorded to Rájpúts, a position which they have been able to maintain as much through the impulse given to Sikhism by the constant demand for soldiers of this class as by the high esteem with which they have been regarded by the British authorities since the Mutiny.

As in most agricultural communities, education among the Jat Sikhs is in a backward condition, though a marked improvement in this respect has been noticeable within the last ten years. The Khatri Sikh, on the other hand, is as a rule quick and well-educated, and his intelligence compares very favourably with that of the slow and rather thick-headed Jat.

Education.

The traditional hatred of the Sikh for the Musalmán went so far as to cause them to object occasionally to the use of the Persian character, and outside the ranks of the village headmen they are almost entirely illiterate. Gúrmúkhi, however, is taught in the village *dharamsálas* by the *Sádh*, and boys can

* For a definition of a Súdra, see page 4.

there learn their letters and how to spell out a passage of the *Granth*, on the payment of a trifling fee by their parents.

The last Census Report shows that the proportion of Sikhs able to read and write only amounts to about 11 per cent. of their total number. Those who enter the army, manage after a time to acquire enough of the Gúrmúkhi character to indite a simple and not easily deciphered epistle to their homes, and to spell out, with difficulty, a similar effusion from their friends. The majority, however, are industrious and painstaking, and show considerable desire for improvement.

Military qualities.

As has already been explained, the virtues of the Jats are identical with those of the Sikhs, but the latter possess in a higher degree the ardent military spirit which had its origin in the warlike precepts of Govind Singh. After the defeat of the *Khálsa* army and the annexation of the Punjáb, Sikhism declined, and the soldier laid aside his sword and musket and returned to the plough. The outbreak of the Mutiny, however, caused an immediate revival of the faith; hundreds of young Jats became Sikhs, and those who but a few years before had proved our stoutest opponents, now joined our ranks and fought for us with a valour and loyalty that is beyond all praise. Since that time service in the army has been eagerly sought after, both in the cavalry and infantry. The Sikh is essentially a fighting man, and his fine qualities are best shown in the army, which is admittedly his natural profession. "Hardy, brave, and of intelligence too slow to understand when he is beaten, obedient to discipline, devotedly attached to his officers, and careless of the caste prohibitions which render so many Hindu races difficult to control and feed in the field, he is unsurpassed as a soldier in the East."* There are many warlike races in India whose military qualities are of a high order, but of these the Sikh indisputably takes the leading place as a thoroughly useful and reliable soldier. Wherever fighting is going on, be it in China, the Straits, Burma, or East Africa, there the Sikh is to be found. Offer him but good pay, and there is no service, however difficult or dangerous, for which he will not gladly come forward.

Value of Sikhism in imbuing the lowest castes with a military spirit.

One of the highest qualities of Sikhism is its power to improve the social condition of its adherents, by removing the trammels of caste. As a Mazbhi Sikh, the despised Chúhra or sweeper at once becomes a valiant and valued soldier, and, imbued with the spirit of his martial faith, loses all memory of his former degraded calling.

---

* Ranjit Singh.—*Lepel Griffin.*

The Sikh is at his best in the infantry. He no doubt becomes an excellent cavalry-soldier with training, but he has not the same aptitude for horsemanship as some of the races which are admittedly his inferiors on foot. In the infantry he is the bravest and steadiest of soldiers. It is part of his creed never to turn his back to his enemy; he has a high opinion of his own military worth; he is stubborn and earnest in action; and while lacking the *élan* and dash of the Pathán, is more faithful, more trustworthy, and far less liable to panic. His qualities are nowhere more conspicuous than in a retreat or defeat, and many distinguished critics consider him to be "equal to any soldier in the world, and superior to any with whom he is likely to come in contact."*

Physique, and sports.

The Jat Sikhs have always been famous for their fine physique and are surpassed by no race in India for high-bred looks, smartness, and soldierly bearing. Their length of limb makes them excellent marchers, and their physical activity is developed by active habits. They are fond of running, jumping, wielding enormous wooden clubs called *múgdars*, and lifting and tossing heavy weights. The younger men are fond of wrestling, and quoit-throwing, the latter a pastime which had fallen into desuetude, but is now much encouraged in the army. The steel *chukra* or quoit, which was invariably worn round the turban, is generally from six to eight inches in diameter, with a razor edge, and properly thrown makes a formidable missile. The Jat Sikh is usually too much occupied with agricultural labour to spare much time for games, and the latter are consequently seldom played, except by the boys of the village, or occasionally at *mélas* or fairs. The most common are *Saunchi* and *Kabbadi*. In *Saunchi* the spectators form a large ring, inside which are two smaller ones. A man from one of these inner rings advances and is chased by two or three men from the other, to elude whom he may trip up, or strike in the chest with the open hand. *Kabbadi* is very much the same as 'Prisoner's Base.' Among the wealthier classes hawking and coursing are still favourite pastimes.

Personal habits and customs.

The Sikh is clean in his personal habits, but does not pay as much attention to his ablutions as a Bráhman or Hindu Rájpút. Before praying he considers it necessary to bathe in *cold* water, so as to render his devotions more acceptable. If prevented by sickness or other causes, he must at least wash his face and hands, and swallow water in view to purification. Twice a day he should fold and unfold his turban, comb his locks, and rinse his mouth. Nudity is held in especial abhorrence and is strictly prohibited. The head should always be covered by a turban, never by a cap, and no food should

* Ranjit Singh.—*Lepel Griffin.*

be taken until after the repetition of the name of the *Gúrú* and the *Jap*, or morning prayer.* When two Sikhs meet, the inferior or younger salutes the other with "*Wah Gúrúji ka Futteh*!" "*Wah Gúrúji ka Khálsa*!" The ordinary Hindu salutation of *Rám Rám* is also occasionally used.

The Jat Sikh is generally a frugal liver. Indeed an inclination to be miserly is one of his chief faults, and he nearly always has a tendency to save at the expense of his food. This love of money, however, is not without its advantages; combined with a spirit of adventure and a taste for fighting, it tempts the Sikh to distant countries and enables us to secure an ample supply of recruits for the Burma Battalions, the Asiatic Artillery, and the Police of Hong Kong and Central Africa. The profits derived from their military service add greatly to the prosperity of the Sikhs; it enables them to tide over the difficulties of bad harvests, and goes far to provide comforts and luxuries which would otherwise be beyond their means. "When he has made a little money, the Jat Sikh often proceeds to invest it by lending to his more needy neighbours, either with or without security, but preferably on mortgage. He lends on land, not so much with the view of making a profit by taking interest, but for the sake of getting more land into his possession and eking out the profits of his own small holdings." The Mazbhi Sikh, on the other hand, is far less penurious than the Jat; he spends his money on meat, tea, and rum, and being but seldom a landowner, has generally less inducements to save.

The dress of the Sikh cultivator is simple in the extreme. The material is almost always unbleached cotton, called *gháti*, made up by the village-weaver from home-grown materials, spun by the women of the family.

Dress.

His clothes consist in the simplest form of three articles—a large turban of coarse cloth, a *dhóti*, or waist-cloth worn round the loins like a kilt, and a *chadar* or wrap thrown over the shoulders. To this might be added a *kúrta* or loose blouse with wide sleeves.†

In winter the jacket is either of woollen cloth or quilted like a *razai*, and it is usual to wear a thick cotton wrap or blanket folded round the body like a plaid. This is coloured and made of superior quality if the wearer is well-to-do. The *kachh* or short drawers, the wearing of which was formerly compulsory among Sikhs, are now seldom seen except among *Kúkas*, *Akális*, and the village greybeards. *Paijámas* or trousers are a hindrance to those who have to labour in the fields, and the wearing of

* The *Jap* or *Jupji* of Gúrú Govind Singh is a supplement of the original *Jupji*, composed by Gúrú Nának. It means literally 'the remembrancer' or 'admonisher,' from *Jap*, to remember,' and was the prayer appointed to be read or repeated in the morning, as it continues to be by pious Sikhs.—History of the Sikhs.—*Cunningham*.

† Hindus and Sikhs button their coats to the *right*, Musalmáns to the *left*.

these garments is usually a sign that the man is either in military service or of superior social position.

The turban or *sáfa* may be white, pink, yellow, red, or blue, and among better classes of Sikhs there is generally an inner *pagri* of a different colour, of which a small triangular portion, called the *pag*,* is generally left showing on the forehead. The well-to-do Jat has his clothes made of better materials, and will generally indulge in a tight-fitting waistcoat, and a black or coloured coat, made of broad cloth or alpaca according to the season.

Ornaments.

Women unless widowed are usually loaded with silver ornaments, and much of the wealth of the family is invested in this manner. Among the men ornaments are rare, as their use is considered a mark of effeminacy, but pensioners who have saved money often invest in a string of gold mohurs worn round the neck, a tighter necklace of gold and coral beads called a *máhla*, or even a pair of gold bangles, called *kangan* which they love to display at marriages and festivals. Money is generally tied in a corner of the wrapper.

Morality and crime.

The mass of the Jat Sikh population may fairly be said to be contented and law-abiding. Crimes of violence are not numerous, and concerted riots are rare. The prevailing crime among them is cattle-lifting and the abduction of married women. Murders, when they occur, usually arise as a consequence of conjugal infidelity, or of quarrels regarding land, crops, and cattle-trespass. The relations of the sexes permit of a good deal of freedom. Immorality is discountenanced by the elders of the villages, and the strong feeling which exists against inter-marriage in the same *gót* is also no doubt a deterrent to debauchery; nevertheless the number of criminal prosecutions arising out of illicit amours and guilty intrigues appear to be steadily increasing. The paucity of women among Jats and Sikhs makes marriage difficult and expensive.† The birth of a daughter, indeed, has come to be regarded as a piece of good-luck, and female infanticide, which is still so common among Rájpúts, has entirely disappeared among the Jats. It is no wonder, therefore, that marriage is regarded as a luxury, and one wife enough for a whole family. "It is almost certain that polyandry is common in practice, and the manner in which the brother claims *karéwa* on the decease of the nominal husband, strongly supports this theory. The girl is considered as purchased by the family, who can seldom afford to pay so large a sum as her price twice over."‡ The Manjha Jat, in fact, has small

* This is survival of the old *Sidha pag* or true Sikh turban which consisted of twelve yards of cloth, and completely protected the head from swordcuts. It is now only worn by old men, and *Kúkas*.

† "The number of single males is nearly double that of single females."—Punjáb Gazetteer.

‡ Ludhiána Gazetteer.

regard for the family honour. "There is undoubtedly a good deal of free intercourse between married women and their brothers-in-law, and in the larger villages immoral relations between the landowners and the women of the *kamin* or menial class are not of unfrequent occurrence.* The customs of Jats and Sikhs with regard to concubinage are also extremely lax, and are encouraged by the *chadar dálna* ceremony by which a man need only put a sheet over a woman's head to make her his lawful wife.

Love of litigation.

A love of litigation appears to be increasing throughout all classes of the agricultural population. Jats and Sikhs are by nature persistent, and never drop a claim, however trivial, which they believe to be based on equity. Law is a matter for which they have no regard and of which they know nothing, except that it will get them all they want if they can get it on their side, and that can only be secured by their swearing everything to be false which their opponents swear to be true. Thus the Jat peasant, who is reasonably frank and truthful in his village, becomes a bold and unscrupulous perjurer as soon as he enters the witness-box.

Food.

The ordinary food of the Sikh peasants consists of *chapátis*, made either with wheat, or barley meal, or with *jowár*, *i.e.*, millet.† These cakes are eaten with *dál* or with a kind of porridge, called *daliya*, prepared from wheat, *jowár*, and *makkai*, the grain being bruised rather than ground and then thrown into a cauldron and boiled with salt and *dál*. Salt is always used, and *mirch* or red pepper is generally added as a seasoning. The whole is washed down by copious draughts of *lassi* or buttermilk. Carrots, turnips, onions, and pumpkins may be eaten, but the favourite substitute for vegetables is *sarsón*, *i.e.*, green gram. Raw milk is seldom drunk, and rice is only used during sickness, at festivals, or by the richer families. Sugar or *gúr* makes its appearance in various forms at marriages and other festive occasions, but like *ghi* is generally regarded as a luxury. Before starting for his daily work, the Sikh will partake of a light meal, generally the leavings of the previous day. If he is well-to-do, he may treat himself to a sweatmeat ball, called *laddu*, made of *gúr*, *til*, and wheatmeal. This is followed by a substantial repast of cakes and *lassi*, which is brought to him in the fields by the women or children when the sun begins to get powerful, and the oxen have their mid-day rest. The heaviest meal is taken in the house at sundown, when the toil of the day is over. The cooking is mostly done by women, but some villages have a *langar-khána* or cook-house where *chapátis* are baked by the Jhinwars during the hot weather.

* Lahore Gazetteer.

† In poorer households the staple food is *berra*, *i.e.*, wheat and gram mixed.

Although the eating of flesh was one of Gúrú Govind's injunctions to his followers, meat is but rarely eaten, and when it is indulged in the animal must be killed by *jhatka, i.e.*, decapitation by a blow at the back of the head. Beef is of course unholy, for the Sikh has an intense veneration for the cow,* but there is no objection to mutton, kid, and goat's flesh, or to that of the wild boar, which, when killed in sport, need not be treated to the *jhatka*.

A Sikh will take food cooked by any orthodox Hindu, or by any other Sikh except a Mazbhi, Chúhra, or Chamár. In theory Sikhism acknowledges no distinctions of caste, but in practice they are more or less admitted. In times of necessity, however, all such restrictions disappear, and food may be eaten even at the hand of Muhammadans. Sikhs of every grade take water without any objection from the *mashaks* and *pakhdls* of Musalmán *bhistis*, and in regiments all feed together in messes, their food being prepared by the *langris* or cooks assisted by the men themselves.

One of the principal objects of Gúrú Govind Singh in instituting the Sikh communion was to remove the restrictions in the matter of food imposed by differences of caste. The *kará parshád* or sacramental food consists of equal portions of flour, sugar, and *ghi*, with a double proportion of water. Any Sikh will eat this at the hands of any other Sikh, except a Mazbhi or a Chamár. *Kará parshád* is much given in charity, and is a standing dish at all religious ceremonies, such as the administering of the *pahúl*, when all present, including those initiated, eat out of the same dish. Those who take the *pahúl* together are called *Gúrbhais*.

The prohibitions against the use of tobacco, which is one of the most important of the rules drawn up by Govind Singh for the guidance of his followers, originated in a desire to preserve them from the gossipping and idle habits engendered by the use of the *huqah*. With Muhammadans and Hindus (except the most high caste Bráhmans) the pipe is always within reach, whatever the work they are doing, and this, no doubt, is a serious check on their industry, and places them at a considerable disadvantage with the Sikhs. The *Gúrú's* injunctions against tobacco, however, have had the effect of encouraging indulgence in narcotics and liquor. The Málwa Sikhs are large consumers of opium and *post*,† while those of the Mánjha have a great partiality for *bhang*, a powerful stimulant extracted from wild hemp. A fondness for liquor and opium is the cause of a good deal of the indebtedness

Indulgence in drugs and liquor.

* "In frontier raids the vanquished Muhammadans would throw themselves at the feet of their conquerors, and putting a tuft of grass in their mouths would appeal for quarter, crying out, "I am your cow."—Ranjit Singh.—*Lepel. Griffin*.

† *Post* is an infusion of poppy heads.

of the Sikh agricultural classes, and illicit cultivation and distillation give rise to many prosecutions on the part of the Revenue authorities.

Sikh cooking utensils are generally made either of brass or *kansi*, *i.e.*, bell-metal, so as to be readily purified by scouring. The only earthen vessels used are the *garha* or water jar, and the *taori* or cooking pot for vegetables. In a regiment the duty of cleaning cooking pots is generally performed by a special class of company servants, called *gúrgas*.

The names of the different cooking utensils and their respective uses are as follows:—

Cooking pots.

Parat, a brass platter in which *atta* is kneaded into *chapatis*.

Gadwa or Lóta, a brass drinking vessel.

Dólni, a larger vessel of the same kind in which water or milk is kept for use.

Batlóhi and *Gágar*, large brass or iron vessels.

Tháli, the brass plate of which food is eaten after it has been cooked.

Táwa, an iron plate on which *chápatis* are baked on the *chula* or hearth.

Kaul and *Katora* or *Béla*, a small brass cup used for drinking milk and *lassi*.

Karchi and *chamcha*, spoons made of brass, wood, or copper used to stir food while it is being cooked.

Chimta, iron tongs used for arranging a fire.

Sandási, an instrument used for lifting a *lota* off the fire.

Handi, a cauldron.

Karáhi, a large iron vessel used for cooking vegetables and *púris*, *i.e.*, *chapátis* made with *ghi* instead of water.

Among Sikhs, as among Jats and other classes of Hindus, the women do not join in the society of the men, and are not admitted to an equality with them. Even when walking together, the woman always follows the man, although there may be no obstacle to their walking abreast. Nevertheless the position of the Sikh woman is undoubtedly higher than that of her Rájpút and Bráhman sisters, for, instead of being secluded and lost for field labour like the latter, she is of great assistance to her husband, and performs a good deal of the lighter kind of agricultural work. The industry of the Jat women is referred to in the proverb of the people: "Of good kind is the Játni who hoe in hand, weeds the fields in company with her husband." Their household duties do not differ from those of females of other classes. Their chief occupation is to grind the corn and cook the food required by their husbands and brothers, to take it out to them in the fields, and to spin cotton. They also milk the cows, gather maize and millet heads, collect fire-wood, pick cotton, boil the milk to be made into *ghi*, sweep out the houses and yards every morning, and make the cattledung into cakes for fuel. To the women also is assigned the duty of drawing water from the wells, as the performance of this office by a man is considered to be very *infra dig*. On the whole, women are treated by their husbands more as servants than as companions. In addition to the occupations already described, they have to play the part of a professional mourner on the death of a relative, by beating their breasts, and wailing for the prescribed period.* The Sikh or Jat woman may not eat in her husband's presence. If he ill-treats her, she cannot get a divorce, and her only chance of happiness is to bear him a son, and thus keep out other rivals for his affection. The dress of the Sikh women is much the same as that of Hindu females of the same class, the only distinction being that they generally have a higher topknot of hair.

Sikh women.

Next to caste, there is no institution in India more permanent than the village community, which dates back to the time of the early Aryan commonwealths. In the Punjáb the headmen of every village are called *Lumbardars*. They are recognized officials, and are directly responsible to the *Zaildár* or *Tahsildar* for the collection of the revenue due from the village and its lands, being assisted by the *Patwári* or village accountant who is responsible for the maintenance and preservation of the records. The typical village almost always divided into wards, called *pattis*, *pannas*, or *thulas*, each *thula* embracing a branch of the clan descended from some common ancestor, and perhaps a few strangers settled by that branch. Each ward is in charge of elders who form the *panchâyat* or village council. Grazing-grounds are held in common; the income derived from grazing dues, hearth-fees, and the rent paid by persons cultivating the common lands, are credited to a general fund; and certain charges, such as the cost of entertaining subordinate officials, travellers, and beggars, are debited to it, forming a primitive system of local self-government. The *panchâyat* settle all questions relating to the general well being of the village, they audit the accounts of the village fund, and all matters affecting the community as a body, such as breaking up jungle land and cutting down trees, must invariably be submitted to their decision. The *zamindars* or landholders

The village community.

*Sikh women were expressly forbidden by Gúrú Govind Singh from making offerings at Hindu or Musalmán shrines, and from taking part in the mourning ceremony above referred to. The rules, however, are more honoured in the breach than in the observance, and Sikh women, now a days, conform in most things to the customs of their Hindu sisters.

consider themselves infinitely superior to the traders and *kamins* or village menials, the distinctive sign of whose inferiority is their liability to pay hearth-fees. Such are the Jat villages. They are communities of clansmen linked sometimes by descent from a common ancestor, sometimes by marriage, sometimes by the fact of a joint foundation of the village. Though often of heterogeneous composition, they are united by close ties, self-supporting, vigorous, and admirably adapted to resist the evil effects of bad seasons, epidemics, and other evils incidental to this country."*

The Punjáb village is almost always composed of houses built of sun-dried bricks or of large clods of caked mud taken from the bottom of a pond. But there are few villages which do not contain one or two masonry houses, the home of a well-to-do headman, of the village moneylender, or perhaps of a pensioned native officer. The houses, crowded as closely as they can be, are separated by narrow winding lanes, only a few feet wide. The houses of a *patti* or ward often lie together and have a separate entrance with a gateway. These gateways in the best Sikh villages are commodious structures, with a roofed shed to the right and left of the entrance, the roof extending over the entrance itself, the foundations of which are raised two or three feet above the level of the pathway. In these travellers are housed, and the owners of the *patti* assemble when the work of the day is over, sitting on the matting spread on the floor, or on the large wooden *takht* or bedstead with which they are generally provided. Between the actual buildings and the cultivated fields is an open space running right round the village, sometimes shaded by *pipal* trees, and almost always in a very insanitary condition. Carts which would take up too much room in the village stand there, and there it is that the cane press will be seen at work in the winter. At one or more sides of the village there are ponds from which earth is excavated for repair of houses, and where cattle are bathed and watered. The backs of the houses are usually blank walls forming an outer boundary to the settlement. In the space running round the village are found the manure heaps, and stacks of cowdung fuel, belonging to each of the households.

The Sikh village.

Entering the village we find the doorways of the houses opening on the main streets, or on side lanes running off them. Ordinarily the front-door leads straight into an open courtyard, with cattle troughs along one or more of its sides. The dwelling-houses will generally be found along the side of the courtyard which fronts the doorway. These are long and narrow, with or without a small verandah in front called a *dalan*, and are

* Report on the Delhi Territories.—*Lord Lawrence.*

generally provided with a flight of steps or a wooden ladder giving access to the roof. Windows there are none; light and air are admitted by the door, and smoke finds its way out by the same way, or perhaps by a hole in the roof. Cooking is carried out for the most part in a partly roofed shelter in a corner of the yard, for the people live as much as they can in the open air, and are only driven indoors by cold or rain. A noticeable object in every house is the large jar-shaped receptacle for grain, called a *bharóla*, made of plastered mud, with a stoppered hole low down in the side by which the grain may run out. Each family living within the enclosure has a separate dwelling-house and cooking-place, while in the yard, outside the doors, much of the available space is taken up by the charpoys and water pots of the household, and the spinning wheels and grindstones of the women. The roof is used for storing heaps of *jowár*, fodder, and bundles of cotton twigs for roofing purposes, also for drying chillies, seed grains, etc., in the sun. Occasionally there is a small upper chamber in the roof, but this is rare. Sometimes the front-door, instead of leading directly into the court, leads into a lodge or *deorhi* out of which a smaller door, placed so that the interior of the yard cannot be seen from the street, leads into the yard itself. The *deorhi* serves as a cart lodge, tool-shed, and stable, and also as a lodging for such guests as are not sufficiently intimate to be taken into the interior of the house. *Deorhis* are only to be found in the houses of well-to-do *zamindárs*, and occasionally have their outer gates ornamented by cornices of carved wood.

Almost every village, and in large communities every *patti* or *thula*, has its guest-house and meeting-place, known as a *dharmsála*. The *dharmsálas* are always kept scrupulously clean, and in most of them a copy of the *Granth* is placed in a window, whence the *Sadhú* or *Granthí* in charge, who is also the village school-master, reads aloud to himself, or to those who have leisure to listen. Fire is kept for the use of such non-Sikh visitors as may wish to smoke, and there is generally a well hard-by. Food and beds are provided for guests by the village headmen, who are supposed to recoup themselves at the expense of the other owners, by levying a small contribution on the land-revenue, or debiting the cost to the *Malba* or village fund.

Family life.

It is a general custom among Jats, subject of course to exceptions, for brothers to live together so long as their father is alive, and to separate at his death. We may thus find four or five brothers, with their families, living in separate houses, ranged round a common courtyard, the whole forming but one household. The usual practice among the yeoman classes, which furnish the majority of our sowárs and sepoys, is for the elder brothers to remain at home, cultivating the ancestral lands, while the younger ones take service in the army and police, and contribute to the family purse by savings from their pay and the pensions granted to them on retirement. The death of a brother often compels a sepoy to ask for his discharge, not from any dissatisfaction with the service, but simply in order to enable him to look after his land. The establishment of an Active Reserve has done much to lessen this difficulty, and has on many occasions enabled the soldier to retain his connection with the army without sacrificing his agricultural interests.

The village money-lender.

Almost every village has its money-lender or *Sahúkár* who is generally a Khatri. He is usually well-treated by the villagers; even those not dependent on him for advances, are civil to him. The money-lenders never bank their money, but keep it circulating in loans as much as possible, or failing this, bury it in the ground. The general rate of interest is two per cent. per month. If disputes arise between the money-lender and his debtors, *pancháyats* or committees of arbitration are sometimes appointed from among the landowners or others of the debtors' class to settle the dispute. But arbitration is now not nearly so freely resorted to as it was in former days. At present the richer Jat proprietors of the Mánjha, who have accumulated wealth from their irrigated land, appear likely to supersede the ordinary money-lending classes in their trade; but they are said to be no easier than the latter in the terms on which they make their loans.

The village menials.

The population of a Sikh village always includes a number of persons of the menial and artizan classes, called *sépis* or *kamins*, who, in return for performing certain customary services, called *sép*, receive from the landlords a certain share of the produce of each harvest. Those whose trade or habits are unobjectionable, such as the Tarkhán (carpenter) or the Nai (barber) live in small houses within the gates; but Chúhras (sweepers) and Chamárs (leather-dressers) being considered unclean, generally have an *abádi* or quarter to themselves situated on the outskirts of the village. An account of most of these classes and their respective functions has been given in Chapter II.

The Jats of the Punjáb have two customs—one known as *chadarband*, the other as *bhaiband*—by which they regulate succession to property. By the first, which is generally practised by Mánjha Sikhs, the property is divided among the mothers; by the second, which is generally in vogue among the Sikhs of the Málwa, the estate is divided in equal shares among the sons. For example, if a man left two widows, one of whom had one son and the other three; by ***chadarband*** the single son of the first widow would take half the estate, and his three half-brothers would each take a sixth. By ***bhaiband*** or ***pagband***, as it is sometimes called, the four sons would each receive a quarter. This, however, does not apply to Bráhman, Khatri, and Rájpút Sikhs who generally adhere to the laws of inheritance customary in their own castes. In the absence of sons, the widow takes a life-interest in the deceased's estate, but where sons succeed, she can only claim a suitable provision. Daughters and their issue cannot inherit, but the former are entitled to maintenance and to be suitably betrothed and married. A widow who remarries loses her rights, even if she marries her husband's brother. A sonless man, or a man whose only son has changed his religion,* can adopt an heir. A boy so adopted counts as a real son even if children are born subsequent to his adoption. The boy to be adopted must be a brother's son, or if there are none available, a cousin in the male line, and no relation in an elder degree than the adopter can be adopted. The ceremony of *godlena* or adoption is as follows. The man seats the boy in his lap (*god*), feeds him with sweetmeats in the presence of the brotherhood, and publicly declares that he has adopted him.

Laws of inheritance.

Pancháyats now play a less important part in the social regulations of the people than they did in former times. A ***pancháyat*** may be described as a court of arbitration for the settlement of disputes, which are also cognisable by law, without having recourse to the courts for justice. It generally consists of from three to five persons, one of whom acts as ***sirpanch*** or chairman, decisions being arrived at by the opinion of the majority. A ***pancháyat*** deals generally with caste matters, and though it has no legal authority, is a powerful tribunal, whose decisions are seldom appealed against. It passes sentences of various degrees of severity. Sometimes the offender is ordered to give a feast to his brotherhood, sometimes to pay a fine,† and if refractory, he may be excluded from social intercourse with his caste fellows. In grave cases he may incur the most terrible penalty of all—total excommunication.

Pancháyats.

No account of an agricultural people would be complete without a brief notice of their system of cultivation. As in most parts of India,

* The change of religion here implied would be conversion to Christianity or Islám. The taking of the *pahúl* or Sikh oath by a Hindu Jat does not affect his position in his family.

† A Sikh who breaks one of the *rahits* or Sikh commandments is required to take the *pahúl* a second time. He must in addition pay a fine which varies in amount from Rs. 5 if the infraction was committed wilfully, to a few annas if it arose through thoughtlessness or ignorance.

there are two crops—one produced in the *rabi* or spring and the other in the *kharif* or autumn. The first consisting of wheat, gram, and barley, is sown in October or November, and harvested in April, May, and June; the second consisting of *jowár* or Indian-corn, is sown in July or August, and harvested in October, November, and December. Maize is planted in July, and sugarcane in March or April. The former is ripe for harvesting by October and the latter ready for cutting in December. The irrigated land generally bears two crops in the year and is seldom allowed to lie fallow; but in districts at a distance from rivers and canals there is a regular rotation of crops, by which portions of the cultivators' lands are given a rest in turn, the soil yielding only two crops in two years. In the highly cultivated canal villages the work of cultivating a holding is incessant, and as wearying to man as to beast. There is no rest in all the twelve months, except for a few days in the rains; and there is so much to do about the months of April to June, and again from October to December, that the cultivator often finds he cannot get through it all, even with the assistance of *atris* or farm-labourers who are generally of the Chúhra class, and thus loses his chance of sowing his *rabi* in time, or neglects some other operation.

Agriculture.

Bullocks are universally used for agricultural work, and he must be a very poor man who can only afford a buffalo, this animal being considered the sign of poverty in a cultivator. The bullocks are either bred in the villages or imported from the great cattle-breeding tracts of the Eastern Punjáb, *i.e.*, Hansi, Hissar, and Rohtak, being brought up in droves by dealers who go from village to village generally a few weeks before the *Baisákhi* and *Diwáli* fairs, and dispose of the surplus at Amritsar and other great centres. The number of milch cattle is not more than sufficient to supply local wants. The milk is boiled and churned in the usual manner. The people of the house use the butter milk or *lassi* which forms a very important part of the cultivators' daily food, but the *ghi* is generally sold or kept for festive occasions, such as marriages, etc. The whole supply, however, is not more than sufficient for the consumption of the wealthier classes.

Horse, cattle, mule, and camel-breeding.

Horse, mule, and camel-breeding receives considerable attention among the Jat Sikhs. It is very common for an enterprising *zamindár* to purchase two or three camels with any savings that he has, and to start in the carrying trade. The Jats are very fond of turning an honest penny in this way; and where carts will not work, camels are most useful for bringing up grain to market.

CHAPTER V.

RECRUITING.

The Sikh recruiting ground.

It has been explained in Chapter II that the Sikh recruiting ground is divided into two portions, known, respectively, as the Mánjha and the Málwa.

The Mánjha.

The Mánjha proper, consists actually of only the portion of land between the Beás and Rávi rivers, and includes the *tahsils* of Amritsar, Taran Taran, Kasúr, and parts of Lahore and Chúnián; but since the time that the Punjáb was taken over, for the sake of convenience, all the country north of the Sutlej has been called the Mánjha. This tract of territory is subdivided into portions known as 'Doábs.' That between the Beás and Rávi is called the Bári Doáb. The country between the Beás and Sutlej, *i.e.*, Kapurthala, Jullundur, and Hoshiarpur, is known as the Doába, the lower portion being called the Jullundur Doáb. The Sikhs coming from this part of the country are called Doába Sikhs. Between the Rávi and Chenáb lies the Rechna Doáb, and between the Chenáb and Jhelum the Chaj Doáb.

The Málwa.

The Málwa is all the country south of the river Sutlej, and includes the districts of Ferozepur and Ludhiána, and the Native States of Patiála, Nábha, Jhind, and Maler Kotla.

Value of the Mánjha.

The Mánjha, though a small tract of country, gives more men to the service than any other portion of the Sikh recruiting ground. The men of the Mánjha rank equally with those of the Málwa as the best Sikh material for military purposes. The Sikhs of the Gujránwála district are closely allied to, and resemble those of the Mánjha, but are not very numerous.

Value of the Málwa.

The Málwa is the largest and most extensive tract. The Sikhs from this part are consequently most numerous; a higher standard of size can be obtained from this portion of the country than from the Mánjha.

Value of the Doába.

The Sikhs of the Doába are not so hardy as those of the Mánjha and Málwa, as they are more absorbed in cultivation. The best men of this tract are found along the Beás and Sutlej, that is, in the southern half of Kapúrthala and in the *tahsil* of Nakodar. In the northern part of the Doába the material is not very good. The Sikhs of the Bári Doáb deteriorate in quality as you advance northward, and the best of them are found in the parts bordering on the Mánjha, *viz.*, the *tahsils* of Ajnala and Batala. The same may be said of the Rechna Doáb, those nearest to the Rávi being the best.

Value of the submontane tracts.

Umballa, Hoshiarpur, Gurdaspur, Sialkót, and Gujrat, that is, the tract of country running along the foot of the Himalayas, is not a good recruiting ground for Sikhs, who, in this portion, are neither numerous nor of very good quality, and, if recruited at all, should be very carefully selected.

In Appendix A, will be found a list of the Sikh districts and *tahsils* with their value as recruiting grounds: this list is compiled from various sources, and the value assigned to each locality takes into consideration both the quantity and quality of Sikhs obtainable; it must however be regarded as merely a rough and approximate estimate.

Head-quarters.

The head-quarters of the recruiting staff officer for Sikhs are fixed at Jullundur; but one of his assistants is generally stationed at Amritsar, which is the religious centre of Sikhism. To assist him in his duties the recruiting staff officer is permanently provided with two assistants.

Recruiting staff.

These officers, who are generally subalterns, are taken from regiments that enlist Sikhs, and are changed every six months. This arrangement has the advantage of enabling a large number of young officers to acquire a knowledge of how recruiting is carried on, and of the classes that provide the best soldiers. They also, by constantly travelling about the country from which the men of their regiments are drawn, obtain a greater insight into their habits, customs, and peculiarities than they could ever hope to pick up in the ordinary course of regimental duty; and as the possession of this knowledge tends to produce a bond of sympathy between the British officer and his men, its acquisition should obviously be encouraged in every possible way. On the other hand, this constant changing of the assistant recruiting officer has its disadvantages, for the probability is that on arrival he knows little about the class of men he has to recruit or the system of working, and just as he has got a fair idea of the people, the country, and the best recruiting grounds, he has to return to his regiment.

System of obtaining recruits.

When a regiment is in want of recruits, the ordinary procedure is for the commanding officer to intimate the fact to the recruiting staff officer, and to detail a party under a native officer or non-commissioned officer, to proceed to the district from which the men are required and to work under the orders of the recruiting officer. It is of great importance that information should, in the first instance, be given as to the particular part of the country from which recruits are required, as the omission to do this is liable to cause considerable delay and inconvenience.

Selection and composition of a recruiting party.

In making the selection of a recruiting party the first consideration is to choose men who belong to the part of the country from which the recruits are required. The *tahsils* or subdivisions of a district are a good guide; for if the men composing the party belong to the *tahsil* in which they are working, they are likely to procure recruits of a good class more readily than men locally unknown. A native officer, who is a man of good position in his own district, should be placed in charge of the party if possible, as his personal influence will be found of great assistance. Should a native officer, however, not be available, a good plan is to send a non-commissioned officer who has hopes of early promotion, as he is more likely to work hard on that account, knowing that a badly chosen batch of recruits, or unnecessary delay in the work, may seriously retard his advancement. In any case not only the commander of the party, but the men as well, should be specially selected for the work they have in hand, and calculated from their position and bearing to give the intending recruit and his family a favourable opinion of the service. This will go a long way towards counteracting the influence of parents, who often are averse to their sons leaving home, and dissuade them from enlisting when the lads themselves are anxious to do so. It is perhaps not inadvisable to let the commander choose his own party, as he is likely to be acquainted with men of his district who possess the necessary qualifications, and being himself responsible for the work, will probably select good assistants. A certain amount of discretion is necessary in judging results; thus a bad harvest may rapidly produce a large number of recruits, while a good year may possibly not give half the number in the same time. Again, in a sickly season a number of the recruits brought in may be disqualified medically and the blame is liable to fall on the recruiting party. The strength of the party will entirely depend on the number of recruits required, but there should always be sufficient to allow of the men working in twos or threes instead of singly.

Method of working.

When the date and place at which the recruiting staff officer wishes the party to report themselves to him have been ascertained, they should be instructed accordingly, and ordered to leave their addresses at the post offices and police stations they pass through. They should also be provided with addressed post-cards, so that they may be able to report progress and communicate with their regiment and the recruiting staff officer. If the party works properly, none of the recruits brought in for inspection should be below the standard of height and chest measurement, nor should they have any very obvious physical defects such as knock-knee, flat feet, or bad varicose veins; should this happen, a disallowance of the money spent on subsistence for such recruits will be pretty sure to prevent a recurrence. Recruiters will sometimes spend the greater part of the time in their villages, and, when only a few days remain, pick up any material that offers and bring it in for inspection. A knowledge that this procedure is likely to result in pecuniary loss to themselves generally acts as a deterrent. Parties cannot usually, however, be held responsible for bringing in recruits who have previously been rejected on medical grounds, as there are men who will offer themselves for enlistment, well knowing that they will not be passed, merely in order to get the subsistence money. The only way to prevent this is to prosecute the individuals if detected doing so more than once. From a month to six weeks at the outside is all that a party should be allowed to stay out, as in that time they will have exhausted their power of producing recruits from the area in which they have influence. The recruiting party should be made absolutely responsible that the men they bring in are of the right class, and what they represent themselves to be. It cannot be too strongly impressed on recruiting parties that a few really good recruits of the right sort are better than a number who only just come up to the required standard.

Rewards for recruiters.

A really good recruiter is invaluable and well worthy of being rewarded, as the duty is by no means an easy one. Every encouragement should be given to men who do well on recruiting duty; an entry to that effect may be made in their sheet rolls, or such other recognition accorded as the commanding officer may consider most suitable, so as to render the duty a popular one. On the other hand, it is perhaps not good policy to punish men who do not give satisfaction, unless they have shown great negligence, as if they see they are liable to punishment, they may not volunteer readily for the duty through fear of failing to do well. The best plan is not to employ such men a second time.

Assistance of civil authorities.

Much assistance can be obtained by notifying the presence of a recruiting party to the civil authorities. *Tahsildars* and *thánadars* can send out messages, give notice in the villages of the date when the party will probably arrive there, and collect *lambardars* and intending recruits.

Disposal of recruits, and medical inspections.

When the recruiting parties have collected their recruits, they take them to the places fixed by the recruiting staff officer for his inspection. Those approved by him are sent with one of the party to the medical officer at Jullundur or to the most conveniently situated station where there is a medical office while the remainder of the party are sent out to collect the balance require if any. The recruiting officer returns to his head-quarters, completes to nominal rolls and documents of the recruits, and despatches those final approved to their regiments.

It is important that recruits should be examined as near to their hom as possible, especially when off the line of railway, as it saves them lo marches and often secures recruits who would not otherwise enlist; it als reduces final rejections to a minimum, and saves rejected men having to return long distances to their homes.

Pay of recruits.

Recruits provisionally enlisted by a party, receive pay from date of provisional enlistment until joining regimental head-quarters, or until date of rejection by the recruiting or medical officers, if they are not finally approved. This is intended to cover feeding, sarai rent, etc. They also get free carriage for their baggage, except in the case of recruits enlisted for silladar cavalry. Rejected recruits are allowed warrants back to their homes, if they can perform the journey by rail or river steamer, with subsistence money, at the rate of two annas a day, for the whole or any portion of the journey which has to be done by road.

Seasons for recruiting.

The best season of the year for recruiting is from the beginning of January until the commencement of the spring harvest, in the middle of April, as during this season there is little work to be done in the fields and the men and boys have plenty of spare time on their hands. After the spring harvest has been gathered in until the sowing of the autumn crops begins, is also a good period, though not so favourable for recruiters, as they have to work in the heat of summer. The worst season is from the beginning of the rains until the middle or end of October, as during this time not only is it difficult to get about the country owing to the swollen state of the rivers and bad condition of the roads, but the men are hard at work preparing the fields for the autumn crop and are not so keen to enlist. The prospect of a long journey in wet weather, over roads knee-deep in slash, is also calculated to prevent lads from coming forward readily for service.

Verification of recruits.

The verification of a recruit's caste and character, unless he happens to be personally known to the recruiting party, depends almost entirely on the village *lambardar*. Though the honesty of the *lambardar* can generally be depended on, it is not absolutely reliable; it is therefore advisable to make the recruiters responsible for these matters, as in that case they will take the trouble to make careful enquiries before enlisting a man. If a recruit should misrepresent his caste and get enlisted, he is sure to be found out sooner or later by the men of his company, but it may be then too late to get rid of him.

When questioning a recruit for the purpose of verification, he should be asked his tribe or *gót*, his caste, *i.e.*, *zát* or *ját*, and the sub-section of the tribe to which he belongs, which is called *muhin* or sometimes *patti*. Captain R. W. Falcon, in his 'Handbook on Sikhs,' states that a recruit will frequently give his tribe when asked his caste, and will not understand the word *got*, though he will answer to his *muhin* or *patti*. He adds that though a man will say he is a *zamindar* or Jat and that he ploughs, to which fact the horniness of the palms of his hands will certify, he may be claiming to be a Jat, without actually being one and without any intention to deceive. Should there be doubts owing to his appearance or to the tribe he gives, he may on being asked acknowledge to being a Jat Kamboh, or Jat Saini or even a Jat Tarkhán or Jat Bráhman, meaning that he has taken to farming, but is not a Jat by birth. The cultivator besides his horny hands has a reddish hue to his skin, sometimes burnt almost to black, while a non-cultivator, unless he happens to be a mechanic, usually has softer hands and a yellowish coloured skin, which latter point is especially the case with Bráhmans. If a Sikh belonging to a good Sikh *tahsil* does not give the name of a well known Jat Sikh tribe, he is usually of some other caste and not a Jat. The wearing of the *khes* does not show for a certainty that a man is a *Singh*, though that probably is the case, for many *Nánakpanthi* Sikhs and even some low caste Hindus now wear it as an ornament. Most *Singhs* wear the Hindu *dhóti*, the respectable and well-to-do ones wearing it down to the feet, while those of a lower class only wear it to the knees. The *kara* or bracelet may be taken as a good sign, though that also is sometimes worn by non-Singhs. *Singhs* now frequently cut their children's hair when young, and sometimes, even in Sikh districts, trim their own beards for appearance sake. The fact of a recruit giving his father's name without the termination *Singh* leads to the supposition that, if not a Hindu, he is probably a *Munna or Sajdhári* Sikh; this point is, however, of more importance in a Hindu or Musalmán than in a Sikh *tahsil*.

The same authority states that the district from which a man comes is more important than his tribe, for though a man coming from a district which is not a purely Sikh one may belong to a good Sikh tribe, it is possible that he may have deteriorated, both through his ancestors having married Hindu wives of the district to which they emigrated, and through the weakening influences of their surroundings.* Another method of recruiting which can be resorted to is to send parties to the various *mélas* or fairs, both religious and

Recruiting at fairs.

*This view is strongly opposed by many Commanding officers, who point out with truth that excellent Sikh recruits are obtainable from non-Sikh districts such as Sialkot and Gurdaspur.

commercial, which are held at many places in all parts of the country, a at almost all seasons of the year. Good recruits are often picked up in the way, as many lads go to them for the very purpose of enlisting, eithe because no parties have been to their districts lately, or because the parents will not allow them to enlist at their homes. The method has is disadvantages, however, the chief among which are, that the recruits offer ing themselves are certain to be unknown to the men, having come from various districts, and it is impossible to verify the description they give themselves, and that, not infrequently, they give the party the slip after having been fed for several days, and cannot then be traced. A list of the principal places where fairs are held in the Sikh districts of the Punjáb, and the times when they take place, is given in Appendix B.

Recruiting by leave and furlough men.

Men returning from furlough and leave may be encouraged to brin back recruits with them, as men thus recruite will probably already have some connectioa with the regiment through their relations, and will therefore take more interest in it. Any sepoys, however, who are given permission to do so, should be clearly warned of the responsibility they incur of having to pay the recruits fares from and to their homes is they should happen to prove unsuitable.

British officers.

The presence of a British officer with the party is a very great advantage and considerably facilitates the work, are it gives the recruits greater confidence if they see an officer under whom they are going to serve. The party also works better under the eye of an officer, and much time is saved by the undesirable recruits being weeded out on the spot, instead of having to wait till they are inspected by the recruiting staff officer. It is, however, unfortunately very seldom possible to spare a British officer for this duty; but those who can obtain leave and accompany a recruiting party in the cold weather would derive much advantage from such a trip by getting to know more about the country from which their men are drawn, and they can at the same time generally obtain a fair amount of sport. To take full advantage of a trip with a recruiting party, an officer should march slowly and make fairly long halts at good centres; he should send out the men of his party in twos and threes to the surrounding villages to advertise his presence and bring in recruits. If he makes the acquaintance of the *zaildar* and *tahsildar* of the district, they will help him by sending out information. Retired native officers will often come a long way to see a British officer, and not infrequently bring in some lads with them who are anxious to enlist.

Regulations.

The regulations on the subject of recruiting are contained in Army Regulations, India, Volume II. Part B.

APPENDIX A.

List of districts and tahsils with their relative value as Sikh recruiting grounds and the names of the principal tribes found therein as shown in the Census Reports.

District.	Tahsils.	Value.	Principal tribes of the district represented among Sikhs.
Amritsar ... (Sikh population, 26,000)	Amritsar ...	Very good ...	Jats, *viz.*—Aulak, Bal, Bat, Bhular, Chahil, Deo, Dháriwál, Dhillon, Gil, Her, Hundal, Khang, Khaire, Man, Pannun, Randháwa, Sandhu, Sansi, Sohal, Sidhu, Uthwal, Virk; also Brahmans; Khatris; Kaláls; Aróras; Tarkháns; Jhinwars; Chhimbas; Mazbhis; Rámdásias, and Chúhras.
	Taran Taran ...	Do. ...	
	Ajnala ...	Fair ...	
*Lahore ... (Sikh population, 132,000.)	Lahore ...	Very good ...	Jats, *viz.*—Bal, Bat, Bhular, Deo, Deswál, Dhaliwál, Dhillon, Gil, Her, Khang, Khosa, Man, Sandhu, Sidhu, Sohal, Virk; also Brahmans; Khatris; Aróras; Kaláls; Kambohs; Mahtams; Labánas; Tarkháns; Chhimbas; Jhinwars; Mazbhis; Rámdásias, and Chúhras.
	Kasur ...	Do. ...	
	Chunian ...	Good ...	
	Sharakpur ...	Bad ...	
Ferozepore ... (Sikh population, 226,000.)	Ferozepore ...	Very good ...	Jats, *viz.*—Bhular, Buta, Dalál, Deswál, Dháliwál, Dhillon, Gil, Her, Man, Sohal, Sandhu, Sidhu, Virk; also Bráhmans; Rájpúts; Khatris; Aróras; Kaláls; Tarkháns; Jhinwars; Chhimbas; Mazbhis; Rámdásias; and Chúhras.
	Moga ...	Do. ...	
	Zira ...	Do. ...	
	Mukhtesar ...	Fair ...	
	Fazilka ...	Bad ...	

* The inhabitants of the Lahore, Kasur, and Chunian tahsils are somewhat addicted to thieving and cattle lifting.

List of districts and tahsils with their relative value as Sikh recruiting grounds, etc.—contd.

District.	Tahsils.	Value.	Principal tribes of the district represented among Sikhs.
Ludhiána ...	Ludhiána ...	Good ...	Jats, *viz.*—Bhular, Chahil, Dagar, Dháriwál, Dhillon, Gharewál, Gil, Her, Sidhu, Uthwal; also Bráhmans; Kaláls; Khatris; Tarkháns; Jhinwars; Rámdásias; and Chúhras.
(Sikh population, 141,000.)	Jagraon ...	Very good ...	
	Samrala ...	Fair ...	
Patiala ...	Patiala ...	Good ...	Jats, *viz.*—Bhular, Chahil, Dháliwál, Dhillon, Gil, Her, Hundal, Man, Sandhu, Sidhu, Sohal, Uthwal; also Bráhmans; Kaláls; Tarkháns; Ramdásias; Mazbhis; Chúhras; Chhimbas; and Jhinwars.
(Sikh population, 285,000.)	Amargarh ...	Very good ...	
	Phul ...	Do. ...	
	Sangrur ...	Good ...	
	Punjour ...	Fair ...	
	Amhadgarh ...	Do. ...	
	Karaingarh ...	Do. ...	
Nabha ...	Nabha ...	Good ...	As in Patiala.
(Sikh population, 63,000.)			
Faridkot ...	Faridkot ...	Very good ...	Jats, *viz.*—Dhillon, Gil, Sohal, Sidhu, Sandhu; also Tarkháns and Chhimbas.
(Sikh population, 47,000.)			

Jullundur ... (Sikh population, 110,000.)	Jullundur ...	Fair ...	Jats, *viz.*—Bains, Bal, Bhular, Deswál, Dháliwál, Dhillon, Gil, Harral, Her, Man, Sohal, Uthwál, Varaich; also Bráhmans; Khatris; Kambohs; Kaláls; Sainis; Mahtams; Jhinwars; Tarkháns; Rámdásias; and Chúhras.
	Nakodar ...	Good ...	
	Phillour ...	Fair ...	
	Nawashahr ...	Do. ...	
Kapurthala ... (Sikh population, 39,000.)	Kapurthala ...	Good ...	Jats, *viz.*—Aulak, Bal, Bhular, Chahil, Chima, Dháliwál, Dhillon, Her, Man, Sohal; also Khatris; Kambohs; Kaláls; Mahtams; and Rámdásias.
Gurdaspur ... (Sikh population, 85,000.)	Gurdaspur ...	Good ...	Jats, *viz.*—Chahil, Dháriwál, Gil, Goraya, Khang, Randháwa, Sindhu; also Rájpúts; Bráhmans; Khatris; Aróras; Kaláls; Sainis; Kambohs; Labánas; Tarkháns; Chhimbas; and Rámdásias.
	Batala ...	Very good ...	
	Shakargarh ...	Fair ...	
	Pathankot ...	Do. ...	
Maler Kotla ... (Sikh population, 7,000.)	Maler Kotla ...	Good ...	Jats, *viz.*—Bhular, Chahil, Dháliwál, Dhillon, Gil, Her, Mán, Sandhu and Sidhu.
Hoshiarpur ... (Sikh population, 70,000.)	Hoshiarpur ...	Fair ...	Jats, *viz.*—Bains, Bhular, Gil, Her, Khang, Man, Sahole, Sindhu, Sohal; also Bráhmans; Rájpúts; Khatris; Mahtams; Sainis; Tarkháns; Chhimbas; Rámdásias; and Mazbhis.
	Dasuya ...	Indifferent ...	
	Garhshankar ...	Fair ...	
	Una ...	Indifferent ...	
Gujranwala ... (Sikh population, 45,000.)	Gujranwala ...	Good ...	Jats, *viz.*—Aulak, Bajwa, Chahil, Chima, Dháriwál, Dhillon, Goraya, Hinjra, Mán, Sánsi, Sidhu, Sindhu, Sekhon, Sohal, Tarar, Varaich, Virk; also Bráhmans; Khatris; Aróras; Labánas; Mahtams; Tarkháns; Chhimbas; Jhinwars; Rámdásias; and Mazbhis.
	Hafizabad ...	Do. ...	
	Wazirabad ...	Fair ...	

List of districts and tahsils with their relative value as Sikh recruiting grounds, etc.—contd.

District.	Tahsils.	Value.	Principal tribes of the district represented among Sikhs.
Umballa ... (Sikh population, 93,000.)	Umballa ...	Fair ...	Jats, *viz* —Bajwa, Bhular, Buta, Chuhil, Ghátwál, Golia, Her, Harral, Jakhar, Mán, Sidhu, Sindhu; also Bráhmans; Sainis; Kaláls; Tarkháns; Jhinwars; Chhimbas; Rámdásias; Mazbhis; and Chúhras.
	Rupar ...	Indifferent ...	
	Kharar ...	Do. ...	
	Naraingarh ...	Do. ...	
	Pipli ...	Bad ...	
	Jagadhri ...	Do. ...	
Jhind ... (Sikh population, 15,000.)	Jhind ...	Good ...	As in Patiala.
Kalsia ... (Sikh population, 7,000.)	Kalsia ...	Indifferent ...	As in Umballa.
	......		
Sialkot ... (Sikh population, 49,000.)	Sialkot ...	Fair ...	Jats, *viz.*—Bajwa, Bains, Bhular, Chahil, Chima, Chaman, Dháriwál, Ghummán, Gil, Goraya, Hingra, Kahlon, Sahi, Sohal, Sidhu and Sindhu; also Rájpúts; Khatris; Labánas; Tarkháns; Chhimbas; Jhinwars; and Rámdásias.
	Raya ...	Good ...	
	Pasrur ...	Do. ...	
	Zafarwal ...	Fair ...	
	Daska ...	Good ...	

Hissar ... (Sikh population, 22,000.)	Hissar ...	Very bad ...	Jats, *viz.*—Aulak, Bal, Chahil, Dalál, Ghátwál, Ghummán, Mán; also Mahtams; and Aróras.
	Hansi ...	Do. ...	
	Biwani ...	Do. ...	
	Sirsa ...	Bad ...	
	Fatehabad ...	Do. ...	
Gujrat ... (Sikh population, 19,000.)	Gujrat ...	Indifferent ...	Jats, *viz.*—Bajwa, Bhular, Buta, Dháriwál, Harral, Mán, Mangat; also Khatris; Labánas; and Aróras.
	Kharian ...	Do. ...	
	Phalia ...	Do. ...	
Karnal ... (Sikh population, 8,000.)	Karnal ...	Very bad ...	Jats, *viz.*—Bajwa, Bal, Bhular, Dháliwál, Ghátwál, Ghummán, Mán, Sandhu; also Ramdasias; Mazbhis; and Chúhras.
	Panipat ...	Do. ...	
	Kaithal ...	Do. ...	
Montgomery ... (Sikh population, 16,000.)	Montgomery ...	Indifferent ...	Jats, *viz.*—Uthwal, Sindhu, Sidhu, Hinjra; also Khatris; Aróras; and Mahtams.
	Gugera ...	Do. ...	
	Dipalpur ...	Do. ...	
	Pak Pattan ...	Do. ...	
Shahpur ... (Sikh population, 9,000.)	Bhera ...	Indifferent ...	Jats, *viz.*—Bains, Bajwa, Buta, Dháriwál, Mahil, Mángat; also Khatris; Aróras; Mazbhis; and Chúhras.
	Shahpur ...	Do. ...	
	Khusháb ...	Do. ...	

List of districts and tahsils with their relative value as Sikh recruiting grounds, etc.—concld.

District.	Tahsils.	Value.	Principal tribes of the district represented among Sikhs.
Jhelum ... (Sikh population, 15,000.)	Jhelum ...	Indifferent ...	Jats, *viz.*—Chahil, Chátta, Chádar, Chima, Dehra, Deo, Ghummán, Khang; also Khatris, and Aróras.
	Chakwal ...	Do. ...	
	Talagang ...	Do. ...	
	Pind Dadan Khan	Do. ...	
Rawal Pindi ... (Sikh population, 27,000.)	Rawal Pindi ...	Indifferent ...	Jats, *viz.*—Chahil, Chima, Dalal, Dehia, Deo, Khang; also Khatris; Rájpúts; and Aróras.
	Attock ...	Do. ...	
	Kuhuta ...	Do. ...	
	Murree ...	Do. ...	
	Pindigheb ...	Do. ...	
	Gujar Khan ...	Do. ...	
	Fatehjang ...	Do. ...	

The Rohtak, Gurgaon, and Delhi districts contain a large population of Jats, but they are essentially Hindus, and Sikhs are practically non-represented among them.

APPENDIX B.

LIST OF PRINCIPAL FAIRS HELD IN THE SIKH RECRUITING DISTRICT.

Mentioned by the Recruiting Staff Officer as affording good opportunities for recruiting. For details of other fairs, see pages 80 to 89 'Sikh and Hindu Festivals.'

Name of District.	Name of Fair.	Where held.	Approximate dates on which held.	REMARKS.
Gujranwala	Lachmanmarri ...	Dhulla ...	18th February and 11th October.	Largely attended by Jats, Sikhs, and Mazbhis.
	Baisakhi ...	Wazirabad ..	11th April ...	Ditto.
	Baddoke ...	Baddoke ...	25th May ...	Ditto.
	Sakhi Sarwar Dhaunkal.	Dhaunkal ...	13th June to 13th July.	Ditto.
	Khangah Dogran Urs.	Khangah Dogran	14th July.	
Ferozepur ...	Maghi ...	Muktsar ...	12th January ...	Largely attended by Jats and Sikhs.
	Baisakhi ...	Nathana ...	12th April ...	Ditto.
	Kakar ...	Manoke ...	End of Har (June-July).	Ditto.
	Tijan ...	Moga ...	Month of Sawan (July-August).	Ditto.
Ludhiana ...	Chet Chaudas ...	Ludhiana ... Machiwara ...	9th and 10th April.	Largely attended by Jat Sikhs.
	Mari ...	Pabbian ...	9th April ...	Ditto.

LIST OF PRINCIPAL FAIRS HELD IN THE SIKH RECRUITING DISTRICT—*contd.*

Mentioned by the Recruiting Staff Officer as affording good opportunities for recruiting. For details of other fairs, see pages 80 to 89, 'Sikh and Hindu Festivals.'

Name of District.	Name of Fair.	Where held.	Approximate dates on which held.	REMARKS.
Ludhiana—*contd.*	Baisakhi ...	Tihara ...	12th April ...	Largely attended by Jat Sikh peasantry.
	Gurusar ...	Kaireke ...	17th April ...	Ditto.
	Bhadlanicha ...	Bhadlanicha ...	15th April ...	Ditto.
	Roshni ...	Ludhiana ...	17th August ...	Ditto.
	Chhapur ...	Chhapur ...	12th to 14th September.	Ditto.
	Gugga ...	Rai Kot ...	15th September ...	Ditto.
Amritsar ...	Chet Chaudas ...	Taran Taran ...	Month of Chet (March-April).	Largely attended by Jat Sikh peasantry.
	Baisakhi ...	Amritsar ...	10th and 11th April	Ditto.
	Dasehra ...	Amritsar ...	September ...	Ditto.
	Diwali ...	Amritsar ...	End of October ...	Ditto.
	Amawasia ...	Taran Taran ...	Every Month ...	Best fair of all for recruiting.
Hoshiarpur	Nandpur Hola ...	Nandpur ...	End of March ...	Largely attended by Jat Sikhs.
	Dehra Sahib ...	Dehra Guru Bhag Singh.	End of March ...	Ditto.
	Rajni ...	Rajni ...	15th March ...	Ditto.
	Baisakhi ...	Dehra Baba Kalsi	11th April ...	Ditto.

LIST OF PRINCIPAL FAIRS HELD IN THE SIKH RECRUITING DISTRICT—*concld.*

Mentioned by the Recruiting Staff Officer as affording good opportunities for recruiting. For details of other fairs, see pages 80 to 89, 'Sikh and Hindu Festivals.'

Name of District.	Name of Fair.	Where held.	Approximate dates on which held.	REMARKS.
Jullundur ...	Chowki ...	Kapurthala ...	15th Phagan (February-March).	Largely attended by Jat Sikh peasantry.
	Baisakhi ...	Kartarpur ...	10th and 11th April	Ditto.
	Jhanda Sahib ...	Khatkara ...	June ..	Ditto.
Lahore ...	Sheoratri ...	Mulapur ...	February-March ...	Largely attended by Jat Sikhs, and offers good opportunities for recruiting.
	Chiraghan ...	Lahore ...	......	Ditto.
	Baisakhi ...	Ram Thaman ...	12th April ...	Ditto.
	Do. ...	Nankana Sahib ...	Do. ...	Ditto.
	Do. ...	Mahomedpur ...	Do. ...	Ditto.
	Do. ...	Fatmal ...	Do. ...	Ditto.
	Samad Bhai Vir Singh.	Pattoke ...	22nd May ...	Ditto.
	Bhadar Kali ...	Niazbeg ...	May-June ...	Ditto.
	Nirjala Ekadasi ...	Nankana Sahib ...	19th June ...	Ditto.
	Dhamkal ...	Shah Dera ...	Sundays in June ...	Ditto.
	Dasehra ...	Lahore ...	September-October	Ditto.
	Tukri ...	Nankana Sahib ...	17th November ...	Ditto.